THE COMPLETE IDIOT'S GUIDE® TO

Playing Percussion

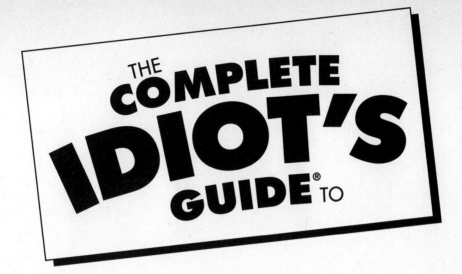

THE COMPLETE IDIOT'S GUIDE® TO

Playing Percussion

by Michael Miller

ALPHA

A member of Penguin Group (USA) Inc.

Dedicated to the memories of George Gaber and Jack Gilfoy: Two dedicated percussionists and educators who will be missed.

ALPHA BOOKS

Published by the Penguin Group

Penguin Group (USA) Inc., 375 Hudson Street, New York, New York 10014, USA

Penguin Group (Canada), 90 Eglinton Avenue East, Suite 700, Toronto, Ontario M4P 2Y3, Canada (a division of Pearson Penguin Canada Inc.)

Penguin Books Ltd., 80 Strand, London WC2R 0RL, England

Penguin Ireland, 25 St. Stephen's Green, Dublin 2, Ireland (a division of Penguin Books Ltd.)

Penguin Group (Australia), 250 Camberwell Road, Camberwell, Victoria 3124, Australia (a division of Pearson Australia Group Pty. Ltd.)

Penguin Books India Pvt. Ltd., 11 Community Centre, Panchsheel Park, New Delhi—110 017, India

Penguin Group (NZ), 67 Apollo Drive, Rosedale, North Shore, Auckland 1311, New Zealand (a division of Pearson New Zealand Ltd.)

Penguin Books (South Africa) (Pty.) Ltd., 24 Sturdee Avenue, Rosebank, Johannesburg 2196, South Africa

Penguin Books Ltd., Registered Offices: 80 Strand, London WC2R 0RL, England

International Standard Book Number: 978-1-59257-929-7
Library of Congress Catalog Card Number: 2009926595

11   10   09   8   7   6   5   4   3   2   1

Interpretation of the printing code: The rightmost number of the first series of numbers is the year of the book's printing; the rightmost number of the second series of numbers is the number of the book's printing. For example, a printing code of 09-1 shows that the first printing occurred in 2009.

Printed in the United States of America

Note: This publication contains the opinions and ideas of its author. It is intended to provide helpful and informative material on the subject matter covered. It is sold with the understanding that the author and publisher are not engaged in rendering professional services in the book. If the reader requires personal assistance or advice, a competent professional should be consulted.

The author and publisher specifically disclaim any responsibility for any liability, loss, or risk, personal or otherwise, which is incurred as a consequence, directly or indirectly, of the use and application of any of the contents of this book.

Most Alpha books are available at special quantity discounts for bulk purchases for sales promotions, premiums, fund-raising, or educational use. Special books, or book excerpts, can also be created to fit specific needs.

For details, write: Special Markets, Alpha Books, 375 Hudson Street, New York, NY 10014.

Publisher: *Marie Butler-Knight*
Editorial Director: *Mike Sanders*
Senior Managing Editor: *Billy Fields*
Acquisitions Editor: *Tom Stevens*
Senior Development Editor: *Phil Kitchel*
Senior Production Editor: *Janette Lynn*
Copy Editor: *Andy Saff*

Cartoonist: *Steve Barr*
Book Designer: *Trina Wurst*
Cover Designer: *Bill Thomas*
Indexer: *Heather McNeill*
Layout: *Brian Massey*
Proofreader: *Laura Caddell*

Contents at a Glance

Contents

Introduction

Back in 2000, I wrote my very first music book, *The Complete Idiot's Guide to Playing Drums*. It was a fun book to write, convinced me that the percussion community is a helpful and friendly one, became one of the best-selling drum books in history, and led me to write another half-dozen or so music books for my friends at Alpha Books. A good experience all around.

Almost a decade later, I tackle another book written for the percussion community, *The Complete Idiot's Guide to Playing Percussion*. The percussion family, after all, is a lot bigger than just the snare drum and drum set; there are literally hundreds of different instruments that you hit, shake, or scrape. And if you're a serious drummer or percussionist, you need to know at least a little about all of them.

Let's face it: I love percussion. I love practicing rudiments on the snare drum and playing fills on the drum set. I love rolling on the timpani and trying, always trying, to master four-mallet technique on the vibes and marimba. I love shaking the tambourine and ringing the triangle and scraping the guiro. I love exploring all the fascinating instruments from other cultures, from the djembe to the tabla. I wish I had a house big enough to hold all the different instruments I love to play.

That's why writing this new book was so fun. I got to explore and play and write about so many interesting instruments, not just the normal drums and cymbals. Every percussion instrument is unique while at the same time similar; it's fun to see what existing technique transfers across instruments and what new skills you need to learn.

And that, I think, is why I was attracted to the percussion family in the first place, all those many years ago: There's always something new. Not to speak negatively of any other musical discipline, but I think it'd get boring playing the same instrument day in and day out. (How do trumpet and flute players do it?) When you're a percussionist, every piece of music is a new opportunity. Today you play the timpani, tomorrow you play the chimes, the day after that you're banging on the bongos and congas. The life of a percussionist is definitely not boring!

That said, learning to play all these different instruments is a bit of a challenge—which is where this book comes in. Whether you're a new player just discovering what's out there or an old hand called upon to do new things, you need a central resource for all the different instruments in the percussion family.

The Complete Idiot's Guide to Playing Percussion is that book—a guide that tells you about and shows you how to play dozens upon dozens of familiar and not yet familiar percussion instruments.

Who This Book Is For

The Complete Idiot's Guide to Playing Percussion is written for both new and experienced percussionists—as well as curious non-percussionists. If you're new to the game, you'll learn a little bit about almost every instrument you might encounter in your musical career—enough so that you won't feel totally lost, anyway. And if you're an experienced player, there's still stuff out there that you're not familiar with, and this book helps you deal with those less common instruments.

For example, you might be a world-class drum set player asked to play in a Latin rhythm section, a first-line snare drummer auditioning for the pit in your school musical, or even an experienced timpanist who has moved over to the main percussion section for a particular piece. In all of these instances, you're likely to encounter instruments that are unfamiliar to you; this book will help you start playing without fumbling around too much.

I've also written this book for non-percussionists—composers, arrangers, conductors, and others who have to interface with the percussion section. *The Complete Idiot's Guide to Playing Percussion* will help you find your way around the instruments of the percussion family—what they do, what they don't do, and how you can use them. It's a nice introduction, even if you never expect to pick up a stick or a mallet in the future.

In other words, I don't expect you to be experienced with or formally trained on all the instruments you read about in this book. (If you were, why would you be reading this book, anyway?) I do assume that you have some musical training, that you know a quarter note from a 16th note and that the key of F has one flat. If you know how to hold a drumstick or timpani mallet, all the better. But you don't have to be a drummer or a timpanist or a master tabla player to figure out what's going on here. This book should help you extend the musical knowledge you have to apply to all the instruments in the percussion family you might encounter.

What You'll Find in This Book

The Complete Idiot's Guide to Playing Percussion describes close to a hundred different percussion instruments—how they work and how to play them. It doesn't have to be read from front to back; in fact, you'll probably find yourself dipping into and out of the book to learn more about specific instruments you encounter.

To that end, I've organized the instruments and information discussed into five major sections.

Part 1, "Welcome to the World of Percussion," starts at the beginning—by discussing what a percussion instrument is, how the percussion family is organized and categorized, and how percussion music is notated.

Part 2, "The World of Concert Percussion," begins our instrument-by-instrument examination of the percussion family, focusing on those instruments used in concert and orchestral music. That includes various types of drums, timpani, cymbals, gongs, mallet instruments, and auxiliary percussion. You'll learn how each instrument works, how these instruments are typically used, and how to play them.

Part 3, "The World of Marching Percussion," presents those percussion instruments used in marching bands and drum corps—snare drums, tenor drums, bass drums, cymbals, and the mallet instruments found in the front line or "pit."

Part 4, "The World of Popular Percussion," starts out with a full chapter on the drum set and then explores the hand drums used in drum circles.

Part 5, "The World of Ethnic Percussion," is a tour of percussion instruments from all around the world, from the congas and surdos of Latin America to the djembes and ashikos of Africa to the doumbeks and tars of the Middle East to the tablas of India to the dagu and taiko of the Far East.

The Complete Idiot's Guide to Playing Percussion concludes with a glossary of percussion instruments and terms, along with a neat little piece for percussion ensemble that demonstrates how the various instruments of the percussion family work and sound together. Feel free to play the piece with your own ensemble if you want!

How to Get the Most Out of This Book

To get the most out of this book, you should know how it is designed. I've tried to put things together to make reading the book and learning how to play the various percussion instruments both fun and easy.

In addition to the main text, you'll find a number of little text boxes that present additional advice and information. These elements enhance your knowledge or point out important pitfalls to avoid, and they look like this:

def•i•ni•tion

These boxes contain definitions of words or terms you'll encounter in the book.

Heads Up

These boxes contain important warnings about what *not* to do when playing an instrument.

Grace Note

These boxes contain additional information about the topic at hand.

Pro Tip

These boxes provide additional tips and advice beyond what's present in the main text.

In addition, you'll see a few icons in the margins, like this one:

 This icon indicates that the instrument discussed in the text is demonstrated on the book's accompanying CD, for you to listen to.

What's on the CD

As I just mentioned, *The Complete Idiot's Guide to Playing Percussion* comes with an accompanying audio CD. You can play this CD in any compact disc player or on your computer.

The CD contains examples of many of the instruments discussed in the book's text. For example, the "Snare Drum" track contains examples of various snare drum techniques, including rolls and rudiments; the "Djembe" track demonstrates examples of the three basic djembe tones. And so on.

The CD concludes with a performance of the percussion ensemble included in Appendix B, *Into the West*. It's a good way to get a handle on how some of these percussion instruments sound when played together.

Let Me Know What You Think

I always love to hear from my readers. Feel free to e-mail me at percussion@ molehillgroup.com. I can't promise that I'll answer every e-mail, but I will promise that I'll read each one!

And, just in case a few mistakes happen to creep into the printed book, you can find a list of any corrections or clarifications on my website (www.molehillgroup. com). That's also where you can find a list of my other books, so feel free to look around—and maybe do a little online shopping!

Acknowledgments

Thanks to the usual suspects at Alpha, including Tom Stevens, Phil Kitchel, Janette Lynn, Andy Saff, Billy Fields, Mike Sanders, and Marie Butler-Knight, for helping to turn my manuscript into a printed book.

Thanks also to all the percussion companies and their representatives who provided the instrument photos used in the book. I'd especially like to thank Steve Armstrong at Pearl, Tad Brown at Pro-Mark, Jim Catalano at Ludwig/Musser Percussion, Sue Kincaid at Remo, Andrew Shreve at Paiste, and Marcia Stevenson at Latin Percussion.

Special Thanks to the Technical Reviewer

The Complete Idiot's Guide to Playing Percussion, like all of my books, was reviewed by an expert who double-checked the accuracy of what you'll learn here and provided additional comments and advice when necessary. The review of this book was conducted by Dr. David Schmalenberger, the assistant head of the Percussion Department at the McNally Smith College of Music in St. Paul, Minnesota.

In addition to his educational duties, David has performed with artists such as John Scofield, Marvin Stamm, Larry Grenadier, Richard Davis, Steve Turre, the Tommy Dorsey Orchestra, Cab Calloway, the Fifth Dimension, and Ernie Krivda. He has recorded with the Garth Alper Trio, the Bigtime Jazz Orchestra, Equilibrium, SCHAG, and the Duluth-Superior Symphony Orchestra, where he was the principal timpanist for 10 years.

David also provided and played many of the instruments you hear on the CD that accompanies this book. (Most tracks were done in one take—great playing, Dave!) I thank David for his review and helpful comments and advice; he helped make this a better book.

Trademarks

All terms mentioned in this book that are known to be or are suspected of being trademarks or service marks have been appropriately capitalized. Alpha Books and Penguin Group (USA) Inc. cannot attest to the accuracy of this information. Use of a term in this book should not be regarded as affecting the validity of any trademark or service mark.

Part 1

Welcome to the World of Percussion

How are percussion instruments categorized? How do you write music for drums and cymbals and such? And just what is a percussion instrument, anyway? This part of the book answers these basic questions and more; it's the place to start learning about those instruments that are part of the percussion family.

A Quick Tour of the Percussion Family

In This Chapter

♦ The history of percussion instruments

♦ How different instruments produce their sounds

♦ Percussion instruments by how they're played

♦ Pitched and indefinite pitched instruments

♦ Percussion instruments by function

♦ Percussion instruments of different cultures

The modern orchestra is divided into several families of instruments. There's the brass family, with its trumpets and trombones and tubas. There's the woodwind family, with the clarinets and oboes and saxophones. There's the string family, of course, with violins and violas and cellos. And then there's the percussion family—an array of instruments both small and large that make more different noises than you can shake a stick at. (And sometimes the noise is made by literally shaking a stick ...)

Just what instruments are part of the percussion family? How do all the various percussion instruments fit together? And how are percussion instruments used in various types of music? All this information—and more—is coming right up.

Getting Friendly with the Percussion Family

What is a percussion instrument? In almost all instances, it's something that you hit or shake. But that's the only commonality; the percussion family is a very large one indeed.

Some percussion instruments, such as a chime or marimba, have a *definite pitch*. Others, such as a cowbell or snare drum, are of *indefinite pitch*. Some instruments have heads, others are solid, and still others are hollow with things inside. Some are tuned high and some are tuned low; some play a single tone while others play multiple tones, some with a range of several octaves.

def•i•ni•tion

> **Definite pitch** is a tone that corresponds to a specific frequency or musical pitch—such as A or E♭. **Indefinite pitch** is a tone that does not correspond to a specific frequency or musical pitch, and is instead a general sound with multiple frequencies.

Where do all these different instruments come from? That's an interesting question, and leads us into a brief but necessary history of the art of percussion.

A Brief History of Percussion

Percussion instruments were likely the first musical instruments in history—or, more precisely, in prehistory. The earliest prehistoric music was primarily vocal, of course, before early humans developed the capacity to make tools and instruments and the like. But once our forebears progressed beyond grunting and humming and whistling, percussionists they became.

Rhythm is in our blood—literally, in the form of the human heartbeat. That may have been the inspiration for early humans supplementing their vocal repertoire with some sort of beat or rhythm, created by pounding one object with the hands or with another object. Or, perhaps, percussion is just an offshoot of the human tendency toward violent behavior—we do like to hit things.

Whatever the driving force, the development of the first percussion instruments evolved hand in hand with the development of man-made tools. This was during the Paleolithic age, around 100,000 years ago. And what were these early percussion instruments? A hollowed-out log, perhaps, or an animal skin stretched over a frame made of bones, maybe even two rocks hit together. The sounds made by these instruments were likely designed to duplicate the rhythmic sounds made by ancient tools, meaning that early percussion music was a kind of work music.

It took a while, but early man eventually moved beyond hitting two bones together to constructing more elaborate percussion instruments—most notably drums, with some sort of animal skin used as a head. The historical record is understandably incomplete, but it's believed that the first shallow-headed log drums were developed around 6000 B.C.E.; we know that small cylindrical drums were discovered in Mesopotamian excavations dating back to 3000 B.C.E.; tomb art indicates that Egyptians used simple percussion instruments in their sacred music circa 2000 B.C.E.; and the Old Testament tells us that the tambourine was used by Hittites circa 1500 B.C.E.

And here's the interesting thing. Unlike other types of musical instruments that developed along more regional lines, percussion instruments were developed by and continue to be used by all major civilizations around the world. Ancient cultures in the Far East, Middle East, Africa, Europe, and the Americas all developed drums and other percussion instruments of various sorts at around the same point on the historical timeline. In most cultures, percussion instruments were used to accompany religious rituals and dances; many cultures relied on drums to signal important events; some tribes in Africa even used drums to imitate human language and thus communicate over long distances.

That said, many of the modern percussion instruments that we use today in Western classical and popular music were first seen in Asia Minor (modern-day Turkey). Thanks to expanding trade routes (and the Crusades), many items from the region were imported into western Europe from the twelfth through the fifteenth centuries. That's one of the few side benefits of a holy war, I guess; the Crusaders brought back to their homelands the drums they found in the Middle East.

One of the first Middle Eastern instruments exported to Europe during this time was a kettledrum called the *naker* or *nakir*, the forefather of today's timpani. The naker was smaller than modern timpani, made from metal or wood shells with goatskin heads. Two drums were typically mounted on horseback, one on either side of the rider. The drums were played as armies marched to war, adding a little bass to the treble of the bugles and trumpets used to rally the troops. Today, of course, the timpani is a mainstay of all orchestral music.

Also coming from this region were cymbals and gongs, as witnessed by the Turkish roots of today's Zildjian family. Other instruments entered the Western repertoire from other regions, such as ancient Romans adopting African drums around 200 B.C.E. and the xylophone emerging from Southeast Asia in the 1300s.

Modern orchestral percussion instruments became standardized in the seventeenth and eighteenth centuries, first with the timpani and cymbals, with other instruments following. During the early 1800s, Ludwig van Beethoven was a major factor in expanding the orchestral percussion; his was among the first works to prominently feature instruments such as crash cymbals, bass drums, and snare drums. And the first orchestral use of the xylophone was in 1874, when French composer Camille Saint-Saens wrote it into the score of *Dance Macabre*.

The first popular drum sets were assembled in the late 1800s, with the invention of the bass drum pedal; this enabled the drummer to play the bass drum with his foot while playing cymbals, snare, and tom-toms with his hands. The hi-hat joined the set in the 1920s, just in time for the jazz era, and the modern-looking set (with smaller bass drum and stand-mounted cymbals) came to the fore in the late 1930s and 1940s.

Of course, things are always evolving. The drum set that Gene Krupa played in the 1930s looks primitive and rather fragile compared to the sets with multiple toms and heavy-duty hardware in use today. Drum construction is much more sophisticated today than it was even a few decades ago, and more and more instruments from other cultures are being introduced into Western classical and popular music. The percussion family just keeps getting bigger—and more interesting.

Types of Percussion Instruments

So now that we know where percussion instruments come from, it's probably time to address a more basic question: Just what instruments fall into the percussion family? Is it just drums and cymbals, or are there other instruments that are also percussive?

Let's start with the obvious and most notable members of the percussion family: drums. A drum is a hollow-body instrument with a membrane head of some sort over the top (and sometimes the bottom). Drums are instruments you hit, with your hand, a stick, or a mallet. Some drums (well, the timpani) have a definite pitch, but most don't.

Then there are cymbals and gongs, thin pieces of round metal that vibrate when hit with a stick or mallet—or when crashed together. Cymbals are used in all types of music, from orchestral to marching to popular, and are available in all sizes, from tiny Turkish finger cymbals to the 20-inch ride cymbals used in rock and jazz to the massive gongs used in orchestral music.

Next up are the mallet instruments—chimes, glockenspiel, marimba, xylophone, and vibes. These instruments have multiple bars arranged like a piano keyboard; each bar vibrates when hit with a mallet, which gives the family its name. As you might suspect, mallet instruments are pitched instruments, with each bar sounding a fixed pitch. Unlike most percussion instruments, mallet instruments can play melodies.

Finally, there's everything else—which is a lot. Aside from drums, cymbals, and mallet instruments, you have all manner of shakers, hand percussion, sound effects, you name it. We're talking cowbells and woodblocks, triangles and tambourines, castanets and maracas. All these little instruments add interesting color to all types of music.

Classifying by How Sounds Are Produced

When looking at how percussion instruments produce sound, there are two primary classes. An *idiophone* is an instrument without a head whose entire body vibrates when struck; a *membranophone* is an instrument with a head that vibrates when struck. In other words, a membranophone is a drum and an idiophone is pretty much everything else, as detailed in the following table.

Percussion Instruments Classified by Sound Production

Classification	Description	Instruments
Idiophone	Entire instrument body vibrates when struck	Bells, chimes, claves, cowbell, cymbals, glockenspiel, gong, marimba, tambourine (headless), triangle, vibraphone, woodblock, xylophone
Membranophone	Membrane or head vibrates when struck	Bass drum, bongos, congas, djembe, snare drum, tabla, tambourine (headed), timbales, timpani, tom-tom

 Grace Note _____

Some music theorists add three more categories to this basic sound classification system. I typically don't include these three classifications as traditional percussion instruments, because they're not, really, at least not as we think of percussion instruments today.

The first supplementary classification is the *chordophone*, where a string vibrates when struck or plucked. This describes exactly how a piano or harpsichord works, which is why some people classify the piano as a percussion instrument. I think that's an overly academic and outmoded classification: Who today thinks of the piano as part of the percussion family? Instead, I think we're better off putting the piano into its own category as a keyboard instrument.

Next up is the *aerophone*, an instrument that produces sound when wind is blown through or around it—a horn, in other words. Naturally, a horn isn't a percussion instrument, but whistles, whips, and sirens might be, depending on how they're used. I'll accept that these few aerophones are sometimes used by percussionists, but call them special cases.

Finally we have the *electrophone*, an instrument that produces sound electronically. For percussive purposes, we're probably talking about drum machines, MIDI instruments, computer loops, and similar things that exist to help non-drummers produce drum parts. While the use of these items is widespread in the popular music of today, they're really beyond the purview of this book. We'll stick to traditional percussion, if you don't mind.

Idiophones

Idiophones produce sounds through the vibration of the entire instrument. These are typically solid-body instruments (such as a cymbal) or instruments constructed from multiple solid-body parts (such as a marimba, which has multiple solid bars). When you hit an idiophone, the entire instrument resonates.

Another way to think of an idiophone is that it's pretty much any percussion instrument that doesn't have a head. So maracas are idiophones, as are all other types of shaker. Instruments you scrape, such as the guiro, are also idiophones.

Most idiophones, however, are instruments you hit. A cymbal is a solid piece of metal that vibrates when you hit it, and is thus an idiophone. So, too, is a triangle, a solid piece of metal that vibrates when struck.

Almost all pitched percussion instruments except the timpani and tabla are idiophones—chimes, marimbas, xylophones, vibes, you name it. With these instruments, you don't have a single vibrating body, but rather multiple vibrating parts; each bar on the marimba keyboard, for example, is a separate vibrating unit.

One interesting instrument that may or may not be an idiophone, depending on its construction, is the tambourine. A traditional headed tambourine is not an idiophone, because the head vibrates when struck with your hand—even though the solid round body (and inserted jingles) also vibrates. But take off the head to create the headless tambourine used in today's pop music, and you have a very definite idiophone; it's that vibrating wood body (and jingles) that makes the sound.

Membranophones

Membranophones are primarily drums. That is, a membranophone is a percussion instrument that has a head, which is pretty much how you define a drum. You hit the head and it makes a sound.

All types of drums classify as membranophones. So a snare drum is a membranophone, as is a bass drum and a tom-tom. Timpani are membranophones, as are tablas, timbales, congas, and djembes. A drum is a drum is a membranophone.

Note that the heads on some membranophones can be tuned to a specific pitch. (Think timpani here, along with some African and Indian drums.) Most membranophones, however, can only be tuned to an approximate or indefinite pitch. So don't expect to tune a snare drum to a perfect C, or a bass drum to a low F. You just can't do it.

Classifying by How They're Played

Another way to classify percussion instruments is by how you play them. You really have just three basic ways to play a percussion instrument: You can hit it with something, you can shake it, or you can scrape it. (Or, in the case of a few rare instruments, you can do all three!)

The following table details which instruments are played in which fashion.

Percussion Instruments Classified by Playing Style

Playing Style	Description	Instruments
Hit	Sound is produced when the instrument is hit with a hand, stick, or mallet	Claves, cowbell, cymbals, drums, mallet instruments (bells, chimes, marimba, vibes, xylophone), tambourine (when hit), triangle
Shake	Sound is produced when the instrument is shaken	Maracas, shekere, tambourine (when shaken), other shakers and rattles
Scrape	Sound is produced when the instrument is scraped with a stick or other item	Guiro, washboard, sandpaper blocks

Things You Hit

Most percussion instruments can be hit in one way or another. (Even instruments you're not supposed to hit will make some sort of noise if you whack them with a large stick!) But here let's concentrate on the ones that are supposed to be hit.

We'll start with drums, of all types, which you hit on the head. Some drums are hit with mallets (timpani and bass drums), some are hit with wooden sticks (snare drums and timbales), still others are hit with your hands (congas, bongos, and most African and Indian drums). Different sounds are produced by hitting the head in different places and with varying techniques; you can also vary the sound by changing the size and type of stick or mallet you use. For example, a much different sound is produced by hitting a tom-tom in the dead center of the head as opposed to striking closer to the rim.

All pitched mallet instruments are also hit, most often with specific types of mallets. A mallet with a harder plastic head will produce a sharper sound than one with a softer yarn head, for example.

In concert and popular music, cymbals and gongs are also hit, with either mallets or sticks. (In orchestral and concert music, this type of cymbal is typically designated as a *suspended cymbal*, as opposed to the two hand cymbals you use for crashes.) Note, however, that you can also scrape a cymbal, to produce a unique effect—although this isn't the standard operating procedure.

Finally, many hand percussion instruments are played by hitting them—either with a beater of some sort (triangle), with your hand (tambourine), or by striking two of the same things together (claves). This latter technique is also used with hand cymbals in both orchestral and marching settings; the two cymbals crash together for a really big sound.

Grace Note

Chimes are hit with something called a mallet, but it's not the same type of long stick-mounted thing you use with marimbas and xylophones. A chime mallet is actually a soft wooden or acrylic hammer.

Pro Tip
If you learn the proper way to hit one type of percussion instrument, you're well on your way to playing all hit instruments. That is, if you can execute rolls and flams and such on a snare drum, those same techniques are also used when playing other drums you hit with sticks or mallets, such as timbales, timpani, and the like. Hand drums require a little different technique, but again, if you can play the congas, you can probably also play bongos and may even be able to figure your way around the djembe. It's the technique that's key.

Things You Shake

Some percussion instruments need to be all shook up to make a sound. Most of these instruments are hollow and have something inside—typically small seeds, beads, or pellets of some sort.

The prototypical shaken instrument is the maracas, essentially hollow gourds with pellets inside. Shake a maraca and the pellets bang around against the inside of the gourd, and you have your expected "ch-ch-ch" shaken kind of sound. For whatever reason, most shaken instruments come from more primitive cultures, and are common in African and Latin music.

Things You Scrape

The final category of percussion technique incorporates those instruments you scrape. This is a rather small category, but it's still worth talking about.

When I think scraped instruments, I think of the guiro. The guiro is a hollow gourd with ridges on the outside; you run a stick or beater of some sort along the ridges to make a scraping sound. Grasshoppers make sounds in a similar way by rubbing their legs together. The sound can be very rhythmic.

Other scraped instruments include sandpaper blocks (two blocks covered with sandpaper that are rubbed together) and washboards (a traditional folk instrument).

Classifying by Pitch (or Lack of Pitch)

Another common way of classifying percussion instruments is by whether or not they can be tuned to a specific pitch or series of pitches. An instrument that has a specific pitch that you can identify on a piano or other melodic instrument is called a *pitched instrument*. An instrument that only sounds a general tone, not an identified pitch, is called an *indefinite pitched instrument*. The next table details which is which.

Percussion Instruments Classified by Pitch

Pitch	Description	Instruments
Definite pitch	Instrument produces a specific pitch or series of pitches	Bells, chimes, glockenspiel, marimba, vibraphone (vibes), timpani, steel drums, tablas
Indefinite pitch	Instrument produces only an approximate tone	Cymbals, most drums (except timpani), shakers, cowbell, claves, etc.

Pitched Percussion

Pitched percussion instruments sound specific pitches and thus can be used to play melodies—or, in some cases, chords. For example, a pitched instrument can play a C that is the same pitch as that note on a piano or violin.

There are two main types of pitched percussion instruments. Mallet instruments, such as the xylophone and marimba, have a series of bars in a piano keyboard–like arrangement, and thus can play multiple pitches (one per bar). Pitched drums, such as the timpani, produce sound like any other drum but are tuned to specific pitches. As you might expect, the mallet instruments are more nimble than are timpani, and they're completely different in context and sound.

The timpani, however, isn't the only drum that can be tuned to a specific pitch. Some Indian drums, such as the tabla, can be pitch-tuned, as can Remo's proprietary Roto Toms. And then there are the steel drums of the Caribbean, with their unique melodic sounds. A steel drum, of course, doesn't have a membrane head; it's constructed from old steel bins, with the bottoms hammered until each spot produces a specific pitch. I suppose a steel drum has more in common with a set of chimes than with a set of timpani, but still—they look like drums, they're called drums, and they're played by drummers. So there.

Grace Note

Technically, a steel drum is an idiophone, as it doesn't have a head and the entire instrument vibrates.

Indefinite Pitched Percussion

Most drums, however, do not sound a specific pitch—no matter what some drummers might think. Log on to any online drumming forum, ask a question about drum tuning, and you'll see some drummer somewhere saying that he tunes his toms to C, A, and F or some similar series of pitches. No matter how well intentioned, these drummers are mistaken: Tom-toms (and snare drums, bass drums, and most other drums) cannot be tuned to precise pitches. While the interval between two drums can approximate a melodic interval ("they're about a third apart"), these intervals aren't exact because the drums' pitches aren't exact.

When you're tuning a drum (timpani excepted, of course), what you're really doing is *tensioning* the drum, not tuning it to a specific pitch. You can make the head tighter or looser, which raises or lowers the drum's fundamental tone, but you can't get it to a specific pitch. They're just not made for that. So you can say that a given drum is tuned high or low, but you can't say it's tuned to an F. It's definitely an indefinite pitch.

Nor do cymbals and gongs, when struck, reproduce exact pitches. Technically, they produce a group of pitches that combine to produce the cymbal's unique sound. If you would look at the acoustical waveform of a cymbal (or any other indefinite pitched instrument), it would look fuzzy and complex, in contrast to the clean and simple waveform of a pitched instrument.

So when you're talking about most percussion instruments (mallet instruments and timpani excepted), they don't sound an exact pitch, nor should they be written to sound an exact pitch. In other words, don't expect a tom-tom or bass drum to substitute for a tuned timpani!

That said, some drums—tom-toms, in particular—can be tensioned to an *approximate* pitch. That is, you can't tune a tom to a perfect C, but you may be able to tune it to something that kind of sort of sounds close to a C. This is best heard relatively, when you have multiple toms tuned to multiple approximate pitches. For example, you may be able to tune a set of four concert toms to pitches that sound a little like C, E, F, and G when heard in relation to each other. In fact, you'll probably run across some orchestral works that notate a specific pitch tuning for concert toms in this fashion.

Know, however, that even though you can tune a drum close to a pitch, the drum really can't produce that exact pitch—at least, not clearly and distinctly. As I noted a few paragraphs back, the acoustical waveform of an indefinite pitched instrument doesn't display the clean pattern required to produce an exact pitch. While the specific frequency for that pitch may be somewhere in the waveform of the indefinite pitched drum, so are lots of other frequencies. It's a "fuzzy" pitch, not a specific pitch, no matter what some people might suppose.

Classifying by Function

Another practical way to classify percussion instruments is by their musical function—that is, in what types of environment they're played. In fact, that's how I've organized the balance of this book, by where and how you're likely to encounter specific instruments.

I've identified three primary types of percussion functions: concert percussion, marching percussion, and popular percussion. A lot of instruments are used in more than one environment; some instruments are used differently in one function than another. The following table provides an overview.

Percussion Instruments by Function

Function	Description	Instruments
Concert percussion	Classical instruments used in a concert or orchestral setting	Bass drum, chimes, concert toms, cymbals (hand or suspended), gong, marimba, orchestra bells, snare drum, timpani, xylophone, vibraphone, various hand percussion (triangle, tambourine, castanets, and so on)
Marching percussion	Portable instruments used in marching bands or drum corps	Bass drum, glockenspiel, snare drum, tenor drums, portable mallet instruments (marimba, xylophone)
Popular percussion	Instruments used in popular music	Drum set, various hand and ethnic percussion (bongos, congas, tambourine, and so on)

Concert Percussion

Most of us (at least those of us in the United States and western Europe) are familiar with traditional concert percussion instruments. Whether you play in an orchestra or concert band, the instruments are pretty much the same. You have the drums (snare drum and bass drum), timpani, cymbals (suspended and hand), mallets (marimba, xylophone, and so on), and an assortment of hand percussion, sometimes called *traps*.

The role of concert percussion is typically support and color. Unlike with marching and popular percussion, which is often used to provide a propulsive beat, concert percussion is more often noted for its absence than its presence. It's the old story of the triangle player who counts through 200 measures of rests, plays one note, and then goes home for the night. It's all about the right note at the right time.

Mallet percussion sometimes plays a greater role, filling in with melodies and countermelodies in certain works. And timpani, of course, plays a dynamic role in much music from the Classical and Romantic periods. But in general, there's a lot of sitting and counting rests while you wait for your moment in the spotlight.

Marching Percussion

Marching percussion is the heartbeat of the marching band and drum corps. There aren't a lot of different instruments, but each instrument typically is played by multiple players. So you'll have a dozen snare drummers, a half-dozen players on tenor drums, three or four bass drummers, a few cymbal players, and so forth. It's all in the service of providing the pulse for the band, the beat that everyone marches to, the cadences that lead the band from one number to the next.

The key marching percussion instrument is the snare drum, of course. We're talking rudimental drumming to the max, full of snappy five- and nine-stroke rolls, flams, paradiddles, and triple ratamacues, all executed with flawless precision. You need real chops, as well as stamina, to play marching percussion these days; you play fast and constantly and at a high volume.

Some marching bands and drum corps now incorporate mallet percussion. We've always had the marching glockenspiel or bells, but now there's often a rolling "pit" that sits at the front of the football field or is dragged along the parade route. Marching xylophones are quite common, as are marimbas. These instruments are used melodically, of course, and don't play all the same cadences that the rest of the section does.

Popular Percussion

Then we have popular percussion, with the signature instrument being the drum set. Popular percussion is what you play in a rock or country or hip hop band; it's also what you play in the pit of a Broadway or school musical. Popular percussion provides the two-and-four backbeat of popular music, the spang-spang-a-lang of jazz and swing, and the four-on-the-floor of disco and dance music.

Popular percussion also includes a bit of color, often in the form of ethnic and hand percussion. That's the girl singer playing tambourine or the guy in the back playing congas; some music has quite a bit of supplemental percussive color, in fact. But this auxiliary percussion is almost always in service to the guy behind the drum set, who is the true rhythmic leader of the band.

Classifying by Culture

Finally, we can look at the percussion family in terms of where each instrument originated or is popular today. This is most useful in terms of world music and ethnic percussion, where different cultures feature different types of instruments.

Interestingly, some instruments are cross-cultural—that is, they may have originated in one culture but have achieved common use in another. The following table details some of the more popular instruments in each culture.

Percussion Instruments by Culture

Culture	Description	Instruments
Western percussion	Traditional concert, marching, and popular instruments	Cymbals, bass drum, snare drum, tom-toms, tenor drums, triangle, tambourine, glockenspiel, marimba, xylophone, vibes, chimes, and so on

Culture	Description	Instruments
Latin percussion	Instruments from Central and South America and the Caribbean	Bongos, conga, timbales, maracas, cowbell, guiro, cabasa, claves, steel drums, cajons, pandiero, berimbaus, cuica, agogo bells
African percussion	Instruments from various African tribes and countries	Djembe, ashiko, djun djun, udu, talking drums, shekere, rattles
Middle Eastern percussion	Instruments from the Arabworld, Israel, and Turkey	Doumbek, tar, tambourines, bendir, rig, finger cymbals, frame drums
Indian percussion	Instruments from India	Tabla, dhol, dholak, khol, mridagnam, pakhawaj, kanjiri
Other Asian percussion	Instruments from China, Japan, Korea, Thailand, and Indonesia	Dagu, zhangu, dalo (gongs), taiko, buk, janggu, yonggo, klong yao, klong kaak, kendang, gender, cheng cheng

Western Percussion

Let's face it; this book is primarily about Western percussion instruments. These are the instruments of the traditional orchestra, concert band, marching band, and rock band. Whether the music is classical or popular, if you're playing it in the United States, you're probably playing a Western percussion instrument.

Which intruments are we talking about? You know them—snare drums and tenor drums, bass drums and timpani, cymbals and gongs, xylophones and marimbas, triangles, and tambourines. These are the intruments with which we're all most familiar.

Not to say that all these instruments originated in the West, of course. Cymbals and timpani come from the Middle East, for example, but have evolved into ubiquitous instruments in Western classical and popular music. But since they're so widely used in our musical culture, we'll call them Western percussion instruments.

Latin Percussion

Latin percussion not only is the name of a big musical instrument company, but also a category of musical instruments that come from Latin America and surrounding regions. We're talking about instruments used in the music of Central America, South America, and the Caribbean—including Cuba and Jamaica.

These instruments are some of the more interesting in the entire percussion family, and most are familiar to Western musicians and listeners. That's because the music of Latin America has become entwined with the European-influenced music of North America. Most audiences are as familiar with reggae and salsa as they are with electronica and the Texas two-step, so we all probably recognize the sound of congas and bongos, claves and cowbells, maracas and guiros. Some of us are also familiar with the unique sounds of Caribbean steel drums, which carry both melody and harmony in their ensembles. These instruments are used in regional music, of course, but also help to flavor much of today's popular and even orchestral music.

African Percussion

Africa is where *Homo sapiens* originated, and also where much of our musical heritage was born. African drums were some of the first drums of note, and remain key to African culture today.

Percussion instruments used throughout Africa include all-wood drums, drums with calf heads, rattles, clappers, cymbals, slit gongs, and bells. Most notable are the djembe and the talking drums of West Africa, along with the ashiko, djun djun, udu, shekere, and various other shakers and rattles.

Middle Eastern Percussion

As noted previously, many of what we view as our traditional Western percussion instruments are actually of Middle Eastern origin. Aside from originating instruments such as cymbals and timpani, the Middle East is also home to some unique percussion instruments such as the doumbek, bendir, tar, rig, and finger cymbals.

Indian Percussion

Percussion in Indian music is perhaps the most unique of all musical cultures. Part of this is due to the complexity of rhythms in Indian music; it's a lot more sophisticated than the simple 4/4 beats that drive our classical, marching, and popular music in the West. Most Indian music is based on a tala, a long and complex rhythmic pattern that is repeated over and over by various percussion instruments, such as the tabla. Other popular percussion instruments in Indian culture include the dhol, dholak, mridangam, khol, and various frame drums.

Other Asian Percussion

Then there's Asia. In China, we have the big dagu bass drums, the smaller zhangu drums, and the dalo (gong). In Japan, there are the traditional taiko drums, even bigger than Chinese dagu. Thailand brings us the klong yao and klong kaak, while Korea contributes buks, yonggos, and janggus. And Indonesia is home to the kendang and gender of the traditional Gamelan ensembles, as well as the unique-looking bonang kettle gongs. There are lots of percussion instruments out there, and they're all quite interesting!

The Least You Need to Know

◆ The first known percussion instruments date back at least 6,000 years; many traditional orchestral percussion instruments were brought to Europe from the Middle East during the Crusades.

◆ Percussion instruments can be classified as idiophones (the entire instrument vibrates) or membranophones (a head vibrates).

◆ Percussion instruments can also be classified by how they're played—hit, shaken, or scraped.

◆ Some percussion instruments (timpani and mallet instruments) sound a definite pitch, while most drums and cymbals are of indefinite pitch.

◆ Different percussion instruments are used in concert, marching, and popular music.

◆ Each region of the world has its own unique percussion instruments—although some cultural cross-pollination takes place.

Chapter 2

A Quick Guide to Percussion Notation

In This Chapter

◆ Notation for pitched percussion instruments

◆ Traditional and alternative notation for indefinite pitched instruments

◆ Special percussion notation

◆ How to interpret longer notes

In many ways, percussion instruments are like any other musical instruments; they play rhythms and (in some cases) pitches that are notated using traditional music notation. But it isn't quite as simple as that. (Is it ever?) Although some percussion instruments are notated on the traditional music staff, others use their own "percussion" staff. And not all percussion instruments are notated with traditional note heads and such.

So how do you write and read music for percussion instruments? That's what this chapter is all about.

Notation for Pitched Instruments

Pitched percussion instruments are easy to write for, as they use traditional pitched music notation. This makes sense, really: If you're playing a middle C that lasts for a quarter note, there's one universal way to write it, no matter which instrument is playing that note.

So whether you're writing for mallet percussion, such as marimba and xylophone, or pitched timpani, the approach is the same: Use the appropriate bass or treble *clef* and write away!

For example, the xylophone is a higher-pitched instrument and is written on the *treble clef*. The timpani, in contrast, is a lower-pitched instrument and is written on the *bass clef*.

def•i•ni•tion

The **clef** signifies a type of musical staff. The **bass clef** is used for lower-pitched instruments, while the **treble clef** is used for higher-pitched instruments.

The xylophone is written on the treble clef.

The timpani is written on the bass clef.

Notation for Non-Pitched Instruments

Writing for non-pitched percussion instruments, such as the snare drum or claves or maracas, is slightly different. Since these instruments do not play specific pitches, you can't designate a pitch for them to play on a traditional staff.

That said, you can assign a line or space on the staff for each instrument, as long as you don't expect that instrument to play that precise pitch. Or you can use a special percussion staff that doesn't have any pitches—which might be the best approach.

Using the Traditional Staff

Let's start by looking at how you use the traditional treble staff to notate indefinite pitched percussion instruments. While it's not technically correct, as these instruments don't have specific pitches, using the treble staff is a fairly common approach, because composers and arrangers are familiar with the staff and it enables them to use traditional staff paper. Just remember that just because a drum or cymbal part is written on a particular line or space, that doesn't mean the instrument will play that pitch.

The key here is to assign a particular instrument to a particular place on the staff. When you're writing one instrument to a staff, it doesn't matter which line or space you use, although something in the middle (A, B, or C) tends to be more readable.

A snare drum part notated on the treble clef.

One advantage to this approach, at least for those who write the music, is that you can notate multiple percussion instruments on a single staff. For example, when writing for a battery of Latin percussion instruments, you might assign the maracas near the top of the staff and the claves near the bottom.

Pro Tip

As it's easier to read parts when the flags are pointing up, you can bend traditional notation rules and force upward flags for notes written on the B or C of the treble clef.

Maracas

Claves

Maracas and claves written on the same staff.

Then there's the instance of composers assigning specific pitches to what are essentially non-pitched instruments. This happens a lot with concert tom-toms, as well as marching tenor drums. As noted in Chapter 1, these drums can be tuned to relative pitches; for example, you can tune four toms to approximate the intervals between the pitches C, E, F, G. This type of relative indefinite pitch obviously confuses some composers into writing specific pitches for the instruments. If you come across a piece like this, play along and tune the drums as close as you can to required notes. It won't be a precise C, for example, but you can probably get it to sound somewhat close.

Heads Up

Writing for three or more instruments on the same staff can be confusing to musicians; the different parts tend to run into one another.

Using the Percussion Staff

Although using a pitched staff for non-pitched instruments is common, especially among composers and arrangers less familiar with percussion instruments, it's not necessarily the right way to do it. The better option is to use a special percussion staff—of which there are two.

The first percussion staff looks like a traditional five-line staff but doesn't have a normal treble or bass clef sign. Instead, there's a special percussion clef sign that looks like a little rectangle. This designates the staff as being of indefinite pitch, and you assign instruments to specific lines and spaces as you would normally.

A five-line percussion staff.

The second type of percussion staff is a single-line staff. With this staff, there's no confusion about playing specific pitches; all that exists is the rhythm.

A single-line percussion staff.

Grace Note _____

Whatever type of staff you use, make sure you spell out the name of the assigned instrument on the very first staff. You then can choose whether to not name each subsequent staff or to use the instrument's abbreviation.

Rhythmic Notation

So when writing for indefinite pitched instruments, you pick a type of staff and assign an instrument to it. Then it's a simple matter of writing the necessary quarter notes and sixteenth notes, right?

Well, it can be. Many composers and arrangers use traditional rhythmic notation when they're writing for percussion. But there's always the option of using special *note heads* instead of traditional note heads, which further specifies that the instrument is playing a rhythm rather than particular pitches.

def•i•ni•tion _____

The **note head** is the round filled or hollow part of the note that designates the note's pitch. The note stem is that part of a note extending up or down from the note head. All notes except whole notes have stems. The flag is that part of the note that extends sideways from the note stem, and is used to designate eighth, sixteenth, and thirty-second notes. An eighth note has one flag, a sixteenth note has two, and a thirty-second note has three.

When might you use these special note heads—typically *x*'s for filled heads and *o*'s for open whole and half note heads? Some arrangers use this type of rhythmic notation for non-drum instruments, such as cymbals, shakers, and the like. In fact, if you're notating for a drum set, it's common to use this type of notation for the ride cymbal, crash cymbal, and hi-hat while maintaining traditional rhythmic notation for the bass drum, snare drum, and tom-toms. You don't have to do it this way, but it's an option.

Special rhythmic notation—x's and o's in place of traditional note heads.

Special Notation

Certain types of percussion have their own unique notation needs, based on the techniques applied to those instruments. We'll look at a few of these special cases here; you'll find more examples when you read about each instrument throughout the balance of this book.

Rolls

Let's start with a special notation used for many types of drums (including both snare drums and timpani) as well as cymbals and pitched mallets. This notation is for the technique known as the *roll*—the rapid alteration of strokes between hands.

On most instruments, there are two types of rolls. The first is called an *open roll* and has a set number of strokes of a set duration (typically thirty-second notes), such as a five-stroke roll on a snare drum. The second type of roll, called a *closed roll*, is more fluid, with the player determining how many strokes played how fast are necessary to fill the notated note length.

To notate an open roll, you add three slash marks to the stem of the key note. You should also designate the number of strokes in the roll, above the roll itself. An open roll typically ends on the following note, and you tie the rolled note together to the ending note. The stroke at the end of the roll is counted as part of the roll, so open rolls are always an odd number (five-stroke, seven-stroke, nine-stroke, and so on).

Notation for an open roll—in this instance, a nine-stroke roll.

A closed roll, such as a buzz roll on a snare drum, doesn't have a designated number of strokes. You notate it similarly to an open roll, with three slash marks on the note stem or above the note head. You do *not* designate the number of strokes above the roll; a closed roll does not have to have an ending note, although many rolls do end with a single tap.

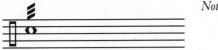

Notation for a closed roll.

So here's the deal. You notate both types of rolls in the same fashion, using three slash marks. If there's a number above the note, the percussionist plays an open roll of that many strokes. If there's no number above the note, the percussionist plays a closed roll of the appropriate duration—unless you're playing a march, in which case the roll is probably open. As you can see, there's some interpretation involved.

Grace Notes

Grace notes are short notes played just ahead of a main note, and are common on all instruments. That's especially the case in the percussion family, where grace notes help create some of the key rudiments for the snare drum. (Learn more about snare drum rudiments in Chapter 8.)

In drumming parlance, a single grace note before a main note is called a *flam*, and is perhaps the most popular snare drum rudiment. Flams are common in not just marching music but also in orchestral and popular music.

A flam—a single grace note.

Two grace notes before a main note are called a *drag*. In most instances, the two grace notes are played on the same hand.

A drag—a double grace note.

Cymbal Notation

As noted previously, cymbals are often written with alternative rhythmic notation. This affords some flexibility when notating special cymbal effects.

For example, if you're notating a ride cymbal part, you use the standard *x*-shaped note heads. But if you want to notate a big crash, use the *o*-shaped note head—either on the same line on the clef or the next space up.

Ride and crash cymbal notation.

Writing a hi-hat part is a little trickier, as the hi-hat can be either open or closed. In this instance, you place a small + above the closed notes and a small ○ above the open notes. It's really easy to get used to, once you gain some experience.

Notating closed and open hi-hats.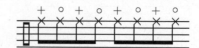

Interpreting Note Length

There's one last thing to discuss in regard to percussion notation, and it requires more interpretation than we've applied so far. It all has to do with how you play a long note on an instrument that is only capable of short ones.

When a composer or arranger notates a whole note for a trumpet or violin, the trumpet player blows or the violinist bows for the entire length of that note. But when a snare drummer sees a whole note, he can't stretch out his stroke; he hits the drum once and the sound fades away quickly—long before the entire whole note is supposed to be done.

That's because the snare drum, like most percussion instruments, doesn't sustain. On a snare drum, all notes sustain the same; it doesn't matter whether you're playing a sixteenth note, quarter note, or whole note, it's the same short *whack*.

So if you're playing a percussion instrument with limited sustain, what do you do when you see a note with a long duration? That's where interpretation comes in. In some instances, you might opt to hit the drum once and let it be. In other instances, however, you might opt to simulate sustain by playing a closed roll for the full duration of the note. This latter approach is common with timpani, where rolling for a whole note is really the sound the composer or arranger wanted, even if he or she didn't know it.

As I said, it's all about interpretation. This means relying on the player's experience, as well as the experience and desires of the conductor or band leader. When in doubt, ask the conductor how he or she wants it played. That way you won't have any surprises!

Of course, if you're playing an instrument with longer sustain—such as a cymbal or triangle—the issue is easier. Just let the instrument sustain through the entire duration of the note. Thus if you're playing a cymbal and see a whole note, you hit the cymbal and let it ring through the full four beats. If you see a quarter note, you let the cymbal ring for only a single beat. Easy!

The Least You Need to Know

- Pitched percussion instruments, such as timpani and mallet instruments, are notated on traditional treble and bass clef staffs.

- Non-pitched percussion instruments can be notated on the traditional staff, a five-line percussion staff, or a one-line percussion staff.

- Some percussion instruments use special rhythmic notation, with *x*'s and *o*'s in place of traditional note heads.

- Certain percussion techniques, such as rolls and flams, require special notation.

- You may need to interpret longer notes as a roll, as most percussion instruments don't have the necessary sustain.

Part 2

The World of Concert Percussion

The variety of percussion instruments used in concert and orchestral music is mind-boggling. The chapters in this part cover all different types of concert percussion instruments: drums, timpani, cymbals and gongs, mallet instruments, and all manner of hand-held auxiliary percussion. Learn what they are—and how to play them!

Drums

In This Chapter

- How concert drums are made

- Getting to know the snare drum

- How to play concert toms

- How Roto Toms work

- Understanding the concert bass drum

We'll start our examination of the percussion family by looking at those instruments used in orchestral and concert music. The first group of instruments we'll look at are the concert drums—snare drums, concert toms, and bass drums.

How Concert Drums Are Made

Whether you're looking at bass drums, tom-toms, or snare drums, all concert drums are similar in construction. You have a round shell of certain depth and thickness with heads on either end. These heads can be plastic (which is most common today) or some sort of animal skin. (For what it's worth, some traditional orchestral players still prefer calf heads, and animal skin heads remain common in various types of world percussion.)

Drum Components

Most drums—snares, toms, and bass drums—have the same component parts. While snare drums add a snare assembly (which we'll discuss later in this chapter) and concert drums forego the bottom head, everything else is pretty much the same from drum to drum.

The component parts of a drum.

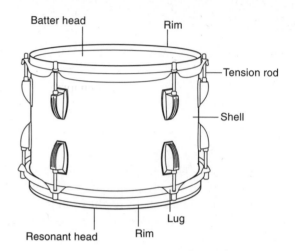

We'll start at the top and work our way down. The first part of the drum is the *batter head*, the thin membrane you strike with a stick or mallet. Modern batter heads are typically made of some sort of plastic, although calfskin heads are still common, especially in orchestral work. The thicker the head, the deeper the head's tone; thinner heads are typically more responsive and thus preferred for delicate orchestral work.

The head is attached to the shell via a wood or metal *rim* that fits the edge of the head to the top of the shell. The rim attaches to the shell via multiple *tension rods*. These tension rods screw into *lugs* that are attached to the shell; you tighten the tension rods to tighten the head and raise the tone of the drum.

Of course, the big part of the drum is the *shell*. The shell should be perfectly round, the better to fit the head. Shells are typically made of wood or metal (or sometimes fiberglass or acrylic); different types of shells have different acoustic properties.

On the bottom of the drum is the *resonant head*, so called because it resonates when the top head is struck. The resonant head can be of the same type as the top head, or made from a thinner material (for more resonance). The resonant head attaches to the shell using the same rim/tension rod/lug assembly.

Shell Size

Drum sizes are normally expressed with the shell depth first and the head/shell diameter second. For example, a snare drum with a 5-inch depth and a 14-inch diameter is described as a 5"×14" drum.

The larger the diameter of the drum, the lower the pitch. So a snare drum, which has a higher pitch, might have a diameter of 14 inches, while a concert bass drum, which has a lower pitch, might have a diameter of 36 inches or so. The depth of the drum also affects the pitch, although not as much as the diameter does. The deeper the drum, the deeper the pitch.

Pro Tip

Shallower drums offer very good sensitivity (the ability to play quietly and still produce a full tone), while deeper drums have a greater low-end range but require more force to generate a full tone.

Shell Materials

Drums can be made of many different materials, from metal to plastic to various types of wood. (This plethora of shell materials is particularly true of snare drums, as we'll examine later in this chapter.) That said, wood is the material of choice for most tom-toms and bass drums and many snares.

Most wood-shelled drums are made of multiple layers—or plies—of wood. Thin shells (typically with four or fewer plies) are quite popular, as they resonate easily and generate a very rich and deep "woody" tone. Medium-thick shells (in the five- or six-ply range) are stiffer and have less vibration but offer greater projection. Thick shells (eight or more plies) don't have as much ring but have really great projection and a higher pitch; they're ideally suited to loud playing in large venues. For that reason, many orchestral players prefer thinner-shelled drums, which produce a more resonant sound.

The wood used in the plies also contributes to the sound of the drum. Maple is the favorite wood of many percussionists, as it produces a fairly even and rich sound across the entire frequency spectrum. Birch drums have a slightly stronger high-frequency response while maintaining a good low-end punch. Mahogany drums produce a warm sound with decent bottom and punch, but less high end.

Some drums are made of shells with different types of wood for each ply. For example, Yamaha makes its concert toms from plies of birch and mahogany; the birch plies provide attack and clarity, while the mahogany plies add warmth to the sound.

Unlike toms and bass drums, snare drums can be made from a variety of materials. It's not unusual to find snare drums with shells of maple, various exotic woods, brass, steel, copper, bronze, carbon fiber, and even titanium. Each material has a distinctive sound, and you have to hear some of these drums to get a good feel for their strengths and weaknesses.

Drum Construction

Beyond the shell itself, another factor in drum construction is the shell's *bearing edge*. This is the edge of the shell upon which the drum head is placed. Rounded bearing edges sound a little different than sharper bearing edges; it's all about how much head touches the shell.

In addition, one has to pay attention to all the hardware attached to the drum. In general, the more a drum vibrates or resonates, the fuller the sound. Anything that keeps a drum from vibrating works to deaden the drum's natural sound. The primary cause of deadening vibrations is the hardware attached to or hanging off the drum. Big, heavy lugs (used to attach the head

Heads Up

Lower-priced drums often have rougher or uneven bearing edges, which can dramatically impact the quality of the drum's sound.

def•i•ni•tion

The **tom mount** is the apparatus that attaches the tom-tom to the stand or tom holder.

and rim to the drum) dampen a lot of vibrations, as do tom-tom holders—especially those that actually poke through the shell of the drum.

To work around this hardware problem, many manufacturers produce low-mass lugs that minimize contact with the drum shell. In addition, so-called suspended *tom mounts* hang toms by their rims or tuning rods, thus avoiding any direct hardware contact with the shell itself.

Introducing the Snare Drum

To many audiences, the most recognized percussion instrument (in the orchestra or otherwise) is the snare drum. Snare drums are common in all types of music—concert, marching, and popular. In fact, the snare drum itself isn't much different from one type of music to another; not only do you have the same elements of construction, you also use a similar technique to play the snare in different scenarios.

Deconstructing a Snare Drum

All snare drums utilize a similar construction, as noted in the following diagram. The top (batter) head is the one you strike with a pair of sticks or brushes; this head is typically coated with a rough finish to facilitate brushwork. The bottom (snare) head is much thinner, to better vibrate the drum's wire snares.

How a snare drum is constructed.

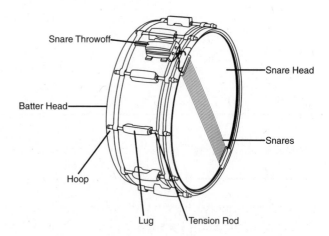

These snare wires give the snare drum its unique sound. Snares are a dozen or more thin metal coils that create a "buzzing" sound when the snare drum is struck. Thinner snare wires create a snappier sound, while thicker snare wires (or those made of other material, such as catgut) produce a deeper, thuddier snare sound.

The snares are typically played tight to the bottom head, but they can also be positioned away from the head; this produces a snareless, tomlike sound. The snares are engaged or disengaged using the *snare throwoff*. The *snare strainer,* which is attached to the throwoff, also facilitates quick and easy tuning of the snares; tighter snares produce a crisper sound, while looser snares produce a buzzier, thicker sound.

Snare drum shells can be made from a variety of woods and metals, each of which produces a slightly different sound, as detailed in the following table. Many orchestral players swear by one type of wood or another, with solid-shell (non-ply) drums in particular favor. That said, metal drums, like Ludwig's vaunted Black Beauty, have a practical versatility; they work equally well in high or low tunings.

> **Pro Tip**
>
> With metal-shell snare drums, hammering of the shell also affects the sound. A hammered shell will tend to have slightly less resonance than a non-hammered shell.

Sound Characteristics of Snare Drum Shells

Shell	Sound
African mahogany	Similar to maple, but with slightly more low end for a warmer tone
Aluminum	Bright with a very open sound and crisp overtones
Birch	Similar to maple, but with slightly less low end and slightly more high end for a harder and brighter tone
Brass	Bright, higher-pitched but with mellow overtones
Bronze	Pleasant midrange sound, capable of being loud and aggressive
Carbon fiber	Similar to fiberglass
Copper	Similar to aluminum, but slightly warmer
Fiberglass	Powerful yet warm, huge crack with sensitive response—like the best of steel and wood drums combined
Lauan (Philippine mahogany)	Similar to maple, but with less high end
Maple (multiple-ply)	Dark and warm
Maple (solid-wood)	Low body, strong midrange focus, solid high-frequency crack
Steel	Powerful yet sensitive, medium pitch and tone, very pronounced ring

As noted previously, the sound of a wood shell drum is also affected by how the shell is constructed. A thinner-shelled drum with fewer plies produces more resonance and a lower pitch than a drum with a thicker shell.

Then there's the option of solid-wood shells, made from a single sheet of wood. Solid-wood snare drums produce a sound that combines low-end warmth with a strong high-end crack, and are valued by many drummers.

Different Types of Snare Drums

The standard size for most orchestral and concert snare drums are 14 inches in diameter. The most common drum depths are 5, 6.5, and 8 inches; some drummers prefer the higher pitch and increased responsiveness of the shallower shell, while others like the fuller sound of the deeper shell.

A Ludwig 6.5"×14" wood shell snare drum.

(Photo courtesy of Ludwig/Musser Percussion.)

def•i•ni•tion

Pianissimo means very soft; **fortissimo** means very loud.

You can use any type of snare drum for concert work, but demanding orchestral players prefer drums that allow extreme fine-tuning of the snare strainer. This provides a greater sensitivity, especially when playing extremely soft passages; you want the same crisp snare sound when playing *pianissimo* as you do when playing *fortissimo*. This type of fine snare adjustment is not present on the types of snare drums sold with most drum kits; you need to upgrade to a specialty orchestral snare to gain this feature.

Grace Note

Most orchestral percussionists own several snare drums of varying sizes and construction. This way they can pull out the right drum for a particular piece of music, no compromises necessary.

Ludwig's 5"×14" Supra-phonic snare drum with Super-Sensitive strainer.

(Photo courtesy of Ludwig/Musser Percussion.)

A 3"×13" piccolo snare drum from Pearl.

(Photo courtesy of Pearl Drums.)

Another popular variation for orchestral work is the *piccolo snare.* A piccolo snare is slightly smaller than a normal snare, in all dimensions. We're talking 12 or 13 inches in diameter, with a typical depth of 3 to 4 inches. Piccolo snares produce a higher-pitched sound with a lot of crack, and have increased sensitivity when compared to normal-sized snares.

> **Pro Tip**
>
> Funk and hip hop drummers sometimes use piccolo snares to produce a back-beat with a tighter "crack" or "pop."

Choosing Your Sticks

In orchestral work, snare drums are played primarily with sticks. Drumsticks are available from a variety of manufacturers; hundreds of different models are available, all with slightly different lengths, diameters, tapers, and beads.

Diagram of a drumstick.

The end of the stick that strikes the drum head is called the *bead.* You can find sticks with all different types and shapes of beads; some are round, some are oval, some are more pointed. In addition, you can buy sticks with either wood or nylon beads. For orchestral snare drum work, wooden beads are more popular; nylon-tip sticks are more for drum set work where you want a brighter sound on the cymbals.

A variety of drumsticks from the Pro-Mark company— from a thick stick with large bead (top) to a thinner model with smaller bead.

(Photo courtesy of Pro-Mark.)

The opposite end of the stick is called the *butt.* A stick is typically straight from the butt to the shoulder, and then tapers down to the bead. Different sticks have different taper angles and shoulder lengths.

The type of wood used to create a drumstick affects the stick's feel, balance, sound, and durability. Most sticks today are made of hickory or maple, both of which have a good combination of strength and weight. Other popular woods for drumsticks include oak, birch, beech, and rosewood.

Drumsticks are typically identified by a number followed by a letter. The number specifies the thickness and weight of the stick, with larger numbers being thinner and lighter. So a 7A is thinner and lighter than a 5A, which is thinner and lighter than a 2A.

Pro Tip

When selecting a stick, look for a good-quality hardwood with the grain running uniformly from butt to bead. It's a good idea to tap the sticks to see if they sound at or near the same relative pitch; otherwise, it's difficult to play them evenly between the hands. You should also roll the sticks on a table or other flat surface to make sure they're not warped—which used to be a bigger problem than it is today.

Pro Tip

You can use any type of stick for any application—you don't have to stick with the suffix recommendations. For example, many jazz drummers use "A" sticks instead of the expected "B" models, just because they like the feel.

The letter following the number—the suffix, as it were—indicates the recommended application for the stick. The "A" suffix is for sticks designed for orchestral work; the "B" suffix is for general rock and pop band work; and the "S" suffix is for "street" applications, such as drum corps and marching bands.

All of this seems straightforward enough until you pick up a few pairs of sticks from a few different manufacturers. What you find then is a noticeable lack of consistency in terms of numbering. For example, a 5A from Pro-Mark isn't quite the same as a 5A from Vic Firth or Regal Tip. In addition, almost every manufacturer offers a variety of proprietary stick models that don't adhere to the general identification system at all. So while you know that a 5A is generally a little thinner and lighter than a 2A, you have no idea where a Pro-Mark 747 or 808 fits in the scheme of things. Nor, for that matter, can you tell if a Vic Firth Buddy Rich model is heavier or lighter than the same company's Steve Gadd model. It can be quite confusing.

With all that said, many orchestral drummers prefer a thinner stick with an "A" suffix, especially when playing softer passages. Thicker sticks are more the province of rock and marching drummers, where volume and durability take precedence over precision—although some orchestral drummers use larger sticks in order to get a more robust tone out of the instrument.

Heads Up

While thin sticks make it easier to play softer passages, they can also sound "thin"—that is, they might not bring out the full sound of the drum, especially with larger drums. It's akin to not having enough breath support on a wind instrument when playing softly; the resulting tone just isn't full enough.

Gripping the Sticks: Matched Grip

When it comes to holding a pair of drumsticks, there are two different approaches—and both are acceptable for use in orchestral and concert music. With *matched grip*, both your hands hold the sticks the same way; the contrasting *traditional grip* requires you to hold your left hand differently from your right.

Matched grip is most widely used in popular music and perfectly acceptable for orchestral music. Since both your hands use an identical grip, this is the easiest grip for beginning drummers to learn. This grip also makes it easier to get around the toms when playing drum set.

To play matched grip, reach out with your hand and grab the stick about a third of the way from the butt end. Grab it with your thumb and the first joint of your index finger, then close your other fingers loosely around the stick. Now turn your wrist so that the back of your hand is facing upward and the stick is angled inward at about a 45-degree angle. Do the same with your other hand, and you're playing matched grip.

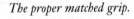

The proper matched grip.

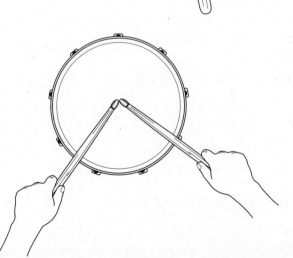

Positioning your hands with matched grip.

Gripping the Sticks: Traditional Grip

With traditional grip, your right hand grips the stick as with matched grip, while your left hand uses a different grip. (For a right-handed individual, that is; it's just the opposite if you're a southpaw.) Some drummers claim more sensitivity when using traditional grip, which makes it the preferred grip for many orchestral or jazz players. However, traditional grip is no better or "more authentic" than matched grip—it's all a matter of which you grew up with or are more comfortable with.

To use traditional grip, remember that only your left hand is different; use the grip described previously for your right hand. Turn your left hand so that your palm is facing up, and then slip the stick between your middle and ring fingers and on through the pocket between your thumb and first finger. There should be about a third of the stick sticking out past your thumb. The stick should rest on your third finger, held in place by your second finger.

Holding the left stick in a traditional grip.

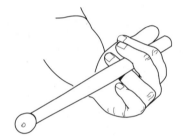

When you play traditional grip, your sticks should form a 90-degree angle on your drumhead. As you can see, your right hand is positioned palm-down, while your left hand is palm-up.

Positioning your hands with traditional grip.

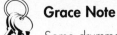

Grace Note _____

Some drummers use a variation on matched grip called *French grip,* where the wrist is turned slightly so that your thumb is on top of the stick. This grip, popular with timpani players, depends more on finger control while promising faster speed and delivering a lighter tone.

Traditional grip originated with marching drummers of old who had to sling their drums over their shoulders. This puts the drum at an angle, with the left side higher than the right. To strike the drumhead properly, drummers had to strike the drum differently with their left hand than with their right—and the traditional grip was born.

Positioning the Snare Drum

Snare drummers in concert bands and orchestras play standing up. As such, the drum should be positioned on a stand tall enough for this purpose. (By the way, not all snare stands are designed for concert use; you may need to add an extension to bring the height up to standing level.)

The snare drum should be positioned roughly at waist level. If you're playing matched grip, the drum should be level horizontally. If you're playing traditional grip, you'll want to angle the drum downward slightly, from left to right.

Playing the Snare Drum

Whether you're playing matched grip or traditional grip, your right-hand stroke is always the same. (Your left hand, naturally, varies by grip.)

The proper matched-grip drum stroke is very simple. Position your stick parallel to the drumhead, with the bead of the stick about three inches off the surface. Now use your wrist (*not* your fingers or your arm!) to snap the stick quickly down to the center of the head and then immediately back up.

Grace Note _____

For more advice and instruction on how to play the snare drum, read my companion book, *The Complete Idiot's Guide to Playing Drums, Second Edition* (Alpha Books, 2004).

This "down-up" motion is your stroke. You should control the stroke in both directions and *not* allow the stick to bounce up of its own volition. It's important that you control the entire stroke; otherwise, you'll be bouncing all over the place and waiting for your stick to return to position.

To make a stroke with your left hand in a traditional grip, you also start with the stick parallel to the head and about three inches off the head. Now use your left wrist to snap the stick down to the head and then back up. It's basically the same "down-up" motion as with matched grip, except that you're doing it by turning your wrist to the right, as opposed to moving your wrist down and then back up.

Heads Up _____

Your natural inclination may be to raise your stick just before you begin the downward stroke. This "up-down-up" stroke is extremely inefficient, can actually slow down your playing, and, when playing at faster tempos, is difficult to control. Work hard to perfect the "down-up" motion *without* an initial upstroke.

The perfect stroke—down and then up.

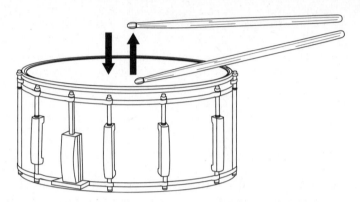

You can control the volume of your stroke in several ways. First, you can begin your stroke from a higher level; hitting the drum from 12 inches away produces a louder note than hitting it from an inch away. Second, you can apply more force to your downstroke; the harder you hit the drum, the louder the note.

Pro Tip
As you play faster, take particular care to play the entire stroke and not let the bounce off the drum dictate the upstroke. Play down and then up with a sharp snap; avoid pressing the stick into the head. The motion, when viewed by an observer, should look like a whip cracking.

Snare Drum Notation

The snare drum is typically noted on either the five-line percussion staff or the traditional treble clef staff, although it can also be notated on the single-line percussion staff. When notated on a five-line staff, the snare drum is typically placed on the third space from the bottom—where you'd find C on the treble clef.

Snare drum notation on a five-line percussion staff—the famous snare drum part from Maurice Ravel's Bolero.

Pro Tip
When writing the snare drum on a five-line staff, you don't have to place the note stems in the down position, which would be expected for third-space placement. (Any note above the middle line typically has note stems pointing downward.) Instead, you can force the note heads up for easier reading.

In some instances, it may be necessary or desired to provide recommended stickings for a particular passage. This tells the drummer which note to play with which hand. For example, if you want the rolling sound of a *paradiddle*, you'd notate a group of sixteenth notes with "RLRR LRLL" sticking—the "R" means right hand and the "L" means left hand. Place the sticking guide directly underneath each note.

Playing a Closed Roll

One of the key tools in the concert drummer's toolbox is the *roll*. A roll is how you get a long note out of an instrument that can play only short notes; you produce a roll by playing lots of short notes really fast, all in a row.

There are two types of rolls you can play: *open rolls* and *closed rolls*. When you play an open roll, you should be able to hear every stroke; it's essentially a series of thirty-second notes, played with double strokes. A closed roll consists of strokes that are hard-pressed into the drumhead. When you press one hand after another fast enough, you shouldn't be able to hear every stroke; this creates the continuous buzz that makes up a closed roll.

Closed rolls are more prevalent in concert and orchestral work. In fact, unless you see a number above the roll indicating the number of strokes, or the roll is written as individual thirty-second notes, assume that you're playing a closed roll. While you still need to play the occasional open roll, the buzz rules in most orchestral music.

As you learned in Chapter 2, all rolls are notated in similar fashion, with three slashes through the note's stem or above the note head. Unless there's a numeric notation above the roll, you should play it as a closed roll.

Notation for a measure-long closed roll.

A closed roll should last the entire length of the note and, unless the roll is tied to an end note, should be ended by lifting from the snare drum rather than hitting a final note. So, for example, if you see a roll above a whole note in a measure of 4/4 time, you should play a closed roll that lasts the entire measure—and no longer. On the other hand, if you see a roll above a whole note tied to a quarter note, play the closed roll for the first measure and then end with a tap on the first beat of the next measure.

Playing an Open Roll

Open rolls are less common in orchestral music than in marching bands and drum corps—although you find a lot of them in concert marches. Unlike a closed roll, where the goal is to create a seamless sound, the notes of an open roll should be heard distinctly, one after another.

Think of an open roll as starting with a group of sixteenth notes. When you play each hand twice in the same space, you're playing double-stroke thirty-second notes. Put another way, instead of playing "RLRL" in sixteenth notes, you're playing "RRLLRRLL" in thirty-second notes. That's all an open roll is—a group of thirty-second notes.

Turn sixteenth notes into a roll by playing each sixteenth note "two for one" with the same hand.

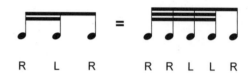

R　　L　　R　　　　　R　R　L　L　R

Open rolls are designated by the number of strokes in the rolls. The name is always an odd number because the final single stroke at the end of the roll is counted as part of the roll. Thus, a roll with four thirty-second notes and a final tap is called a five-stroke roll; one with eight thirty-second notes and a final tap is called a nine-stroke roll. The following figure shows the different open rolls—how they're commonly written and how they're actually played.

Pro Tip
Some drum instructors say you should bounce your double strokes, and they might call an open roll a "bounce roll." While that approach is valid, it's one I personally disagree with, especially in orchestral applications. Even though you're playing double strokes (two rights or two lefts), which would be easy to do by letting your stick bounce off the head, a true open roll is created by playing each stroke separately, in a controlled fashion. So when you play "RRLL," you actually *play* two rights, followed by two lefts. This will produce a very clean, very distinct, very controlled sound. Of course, when you increase the tempo, bouncing is probably unavoidable—and many drummers bounce their rolls even at slower tempos. Like a lot of drumming techniques, there is no single correct way to do it—although I definitely prefer maintaining as much stick control as possible.

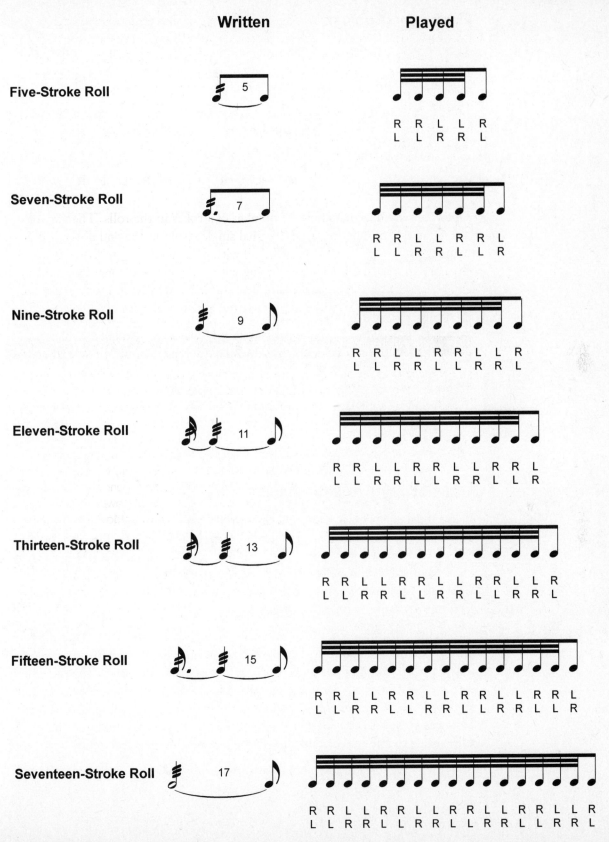

Open stroke rolls.

Playing Grace Notes

A *grace note* is a short note that you play immediately preceding a regular note. Typically the grace note (or notes—you can play more than one) is played shorter and softer than the main note and leads you into the primary note.

This leads us to the drum technique known as the *flam*—a grace note played just before a main note. The grace note is played lighter and tight up against the second, primary note, which can be of any duration.

Grace Note _____

The name *flam* comes from the sound of the pattern. When you play the two notes properly, it makes a sound like "fa-lam!" In fact, the way to learn this technique is to start with the two notes spaced wide apart ("fa——lam") and then gradually decrease the space between the notes, until you get the "flam" sound.

If one grace note is good, two is even better. Playing two grace notes before the main note is called a *drag.* The grace notes are played with double strokes, in either "LL-R" or "RR-L" stickings.

A flam and a drag.

Flam   Drag

Advanced Snare Drum Technique

We've touched on only the bare minimum of snare drum techniques, especially for orchestral purposes. A talented orchestral snare drummer typically has years and years of training under his belt; he's been through all the method books, learned all the rudiments, and played all of the relevant repertoire. That's because orchestral snare drumming requires the utmost of technique from the drummer; it's a tough gig.

If marching drumming is all about speed and precision, and rock drumming is all about volume and feel, then orchestral snare drumming is all about sensitivity. You'll encounter passages that require fast execution at low volume levels; extreme contrasts in dynamics, from very loud to very soft at the drop of a dime; and use of all the rudiments and more in difficult-to-play rhythmic patterns. You need to be able to read anything put in front of you, without questioning, and be able to follow the conductor through multiple time and tempo changes.

Like I said, it's a tough gig—but a very rewarding one.

Introducing Concert Toms

If the snare drum is the soprano voice of the concert percussion section and the bass drum is, well, the bass voice, the tenor voice is provided by a set of concert toms. Concert toms are commonly used to provide a "jungle" effect, although some composers and arrangers utilize the toms more creatively.

By the way, concert toms are not unique to concert music. They're also used in popular music, to add multiple toms to a standard drum set. And with marching percussion, quad tenor drums fill the same role the concert toms fill in orchestral music.

Understanding Concert Toms

A concert tom is a single-headed wood tom-tom, as opposed to the double-headed toms typically found on today's drum sets. And, unlike a snare drum, concert toms don't have vibrating metal snares; this makes for a deeper, thuddier sound, in contrast to the snare drum's crisp, cutting sound.

A typical set of concert toms consists of either four or eight individual drums, arranged from left to right in terms of size—the larger drums to the left leading to the smaller drums on the right, just as with timpani. Concert toms are typically attached two per floor stand.

Grace Note _____

One of the first drummers to use concert toms on a popular recording was L.A. session drummer Hal Blaine. His custom-made fiberglass toms ultimately evolved into Ludwig's Octa-plus set.

Grace Note _____

While most concert toms are single-headed, Pearl makes a line of double-headed concert toms. In theory, a double-headed tom will have more ring than a single-headed model.

A set of eight concert toms.

(Photo courtesy of Pearl Drums.)

Playing Concert Toms

Concert toms can be played with regular drum sticks or timpani mallets. Sticks provide a brighter sound, while softer felt mallets provide a more traditional ringing thud and are more common in orchestral work.

Arrange the toms in front of you so that all four or eight are within easy reach while you are standing; you want to be able to execute a flawless run down the drums without breaking your stance. You can arrange the drums in a straight line or stagger them like the white and black keys on a piano; this latter approach is a good idea if you have a larger set of toms.

When playing concert toms, hold your sticks or mallets with either matched grip or the similar French grip—the same way you'd hold timpani mallets. Unlike with timpani, you hit the concert toms dead center.

Notating Concert Toms

Writing and reading music for concert toms aren't that difficult. Even though the drums are non-pitched, you use the treble or bass clef staff and assign each tom a specific space or line. It's easy enough to fit eight concert toms on a standard staff in this method. Play the tom assigned to a specific pitch.

In some instances, the composer or arranger will request that the toms be tuned to specific notes. As we've discussed, you really can't do that; concert toms are indefinite pitched instruments. Still, you can probably tune the toms close to the notes requested, at least enough so that you can hear the relative intervals between the notes. That is, if a piece dictates toms tuned to C, E, F, and G, you can tune the first drum as close as you can to a true C, then tune the second drum a major third higher than the first, the third drum a minor second above that, and the fourth drum a major second above that. Close is as good as you can get—but it might be good enough to let you play simple melodies on the toms.

Introducing Roto Toms

Similar to concert toms is the unique instrument called the *Roto Tom*. A Roto Tom is a drum without a shell that can be tuned to a specific pitch; it is typically used for special effects in orchestral music.

How Roto Toms Work

As noted, a Roto Tom is a tom without a traditional shell. A Roto Tom is essentially a single head attached to a metal frame. The head is tuned by rotating the frame; this increases or decreases the head tension. Rotate the frame clockwise for a higher pitch or counterclockwise for a lower pitch.

Unlike traditional concert toms, the Roto Tom can be tuned to a specific pitch. Roto Toms are typically found in groups of two or more. Remo currently sells Roto Toms in 14-, 12-, 10-, 8-, and 6-inch sizes. You can assemble as many or as few Roto Toms as needed for a given ensemble or piece.

A set of three Remo Roto Toms.

(Photo courtesy of Remo, Inc.)

As for pitch, each Roto Tom has a fairly wide range—an octave per drum. The sound is a little pinched at the top of the range and a little flabby at the bottom; the middle notes are more full with better sustain.

Roto Toms sound much deeper than you'd expect, especially in the larger sizes. In fact, larger Roto Toms sound remarkably like timpani—and, in many cases, are used to substitute for timpani during practice and when budget or situational constraints prohibit use of the larger drums.

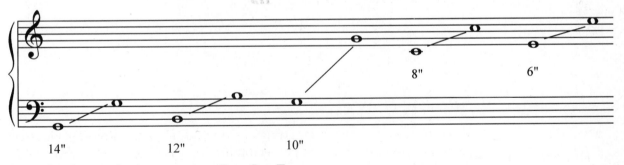

Practical pitch ranges for the most common Remo Roto Toms.

Grace Note _____

Roto Toms can also substitute for timpani in playing very high parts, where a piccolo timpani might otherwise be called for—or for notes above the practical range of a piccolo timp.

Playing Roto Toms

Roto Toms are typically played while standing. The drummer uses traditional drumsticks or timpani mallets. Unlike concert toms, Roto Toms sound better when played with thinner sticks, due to the size of the head and lack of depth. Mallets provide a softer, more melodic sound.

Since you can quickly and easily tune Roto Toms to a specific pitch, it's not unusual to find pitch changes throughout the course of a piece, much as you have with timpani music. When you see a pitch change coming, get ready to rotate the drum to the new pitch.

Introducing the Concert Bass Drum

 It seems that virtually every type of music uses the bass drum—the bottom voice of the percussion family. Unlike popular music, where the bass drum is played with a pedal, the concert bass drum is played by a standing player using a mallet.

Understanding Concert Bass Drums

Concert bass drums are typically large drums. Sizes do vary, of course, with head diameters ranging from 28 to 40 inches; drum depth varies along with the head diameter. The most common concert bass drum sizes are 28"×14" deep, 32"×16", and 36"×18".

A concert bass drum on a suspended mount.

(Photo courtesy of Ludwig/Musser Percussion.)

A concert bass drum can be placed on top of a folding stand with padding on top. This places the drum in a fixed vertical position, with the batter head to the right of the player.

It's also common to mount the bass drum on a suspension cradle, which can then be rotated to any angle. In this type of setup, the drum is typically rotated about 45 degrees, for ease of playing—with the batter head up, of course.

When tuning a concert bass drum, set the tension of the resonant head about a major second higher than the batter head. You want to achieve a full tone, not a dampened one, for best effect.

Playing the Bass Drum

The concert bass drum is played with one or two large padded mallets. In most instances, you play the drum one-handed, with the mallet held in the right hand; your left hand is used to muffle the drum. If the music dictates two mallets (for a roll, for example), you use your right knee or forearm to muffle the drum—or place an external muffling device on the drum head.

Unlike with concert toms, you typically don't strike the bass drum in the center of the head; this produces too muffled a tone. Instead, strike a few inches off-center—close to the center, but not quite there. Use a direct, not a glancing stroke, but don't bury the mallet in the head (unless you're striving for a highly muffled effect, that is).

Let the bass drum ring for the duration of the written note, then muffle the drum with your hand or leg to stop the ring. For staccato notes, muffle the drum simultaneous with the batter stroke.

Pro Tip
For a more legato sound, use a longer stroke. For staccato notes, use a shorter, more direct stroke.

Bass drum mallets can be padded with felt or wool. You can also use unpadded wood or plastic mallets for a brighter, more percussive sound. Use a larger batter for a larger drum.

A selection of bass drum mallets.

(Photo courtesy of Ludwig/Musser Percussion.)

Notating the Bass Drum

The concert bass drum part can be written on its own staff or on a staff shared with other instruments. On its own, it's typically the bottom space of the percussion staff or the bass clef staff. When sharing a staff, it is typically written on the first space below the staff.

A typical bass drum part, from Sergei Prokofiev's Violin Concerto No. 2 in G Minor.

Bass drum notation is similar to snare drum notation, but without the sticking—and typically without flams. Rolls are common and are notated with the traditional slash notation; consider all bass drum rolls to be closed rolls, or as close to closed as you can get while playing single strokes.

The Least You Need to Know

♦ Drums can be made from solid wood shells, multi-ply wood shells, or various types of metal.

♦ The snare drum is the soprano voice of the concert percussion section; the unique buzzing sound comes from the metal snares underneath the resonant head.

♦ Snare drum sticks can be held in either matched grip (both hands the same) or traditional grip (the left stick positioned between your middle fingers and thumb).

♦ Concert toms are a group of four to eight headless tom-toms, typically used for "jungle" effects.

♦ Roto Toms are single-headed drums without shells that can be tuned to specific pitches.

♦ The concert bass drum is a large (typically 36- to 40-inch) bass drum mounted on a stand and played with a padded beater.

Chapter 4

Timpani

In This Chapter

◆ What makes timpani unique (hint: it's the tuning)

◆ The history of the timpani

◆ The parts of the modern timpani

◆ All about timpani mallets

◆ How to tune and play the timpani

Even more important than the snare drum for orchestral work is the timpani. Every orchestra and concert band in the land has a timpani player on call, mallets in hand, just waiting to let forth with a thunderous roll.

Composers have been writing for timpani since Bach's day, and most major symphonies of the Classical and Romantic periods have essential and often quite interesting timpani parts. It goes without saying that most serious percussionists will find themselves behind the big copper drums at some point in their careers, which makes knowledge of the timpani essential.

Getting to Know the Timpani

Timpani are large, copper-shelled drums with plastic or calfskin heads that sound at the low end of the percussion range, almost like the sound of thunder. Timpani can play a supporting role, like the other percussion instruments, or a lead role. Timpani can double other low-pitched instruments, such as basses and trombones, or play a melodic line by themselves.

Undampened, the timpani has a short sustain, almost like a pitched bass drum. Staccato notes are accomplished by manually damping the head with the hand. Longer sustain is accomplished by two-handed rolling, typically on a single drum.

What makes timpani different from most other drums is that timpani can be tuned to precise musical notes. That's right, timpani are definite pitched instruments, each drum with a range of about a fifth; for example, a 29-inch timpani can be tuned from F to C. Put multiple drums together and you get a range of possible notes that reach over an octave and a half.

32"   29"   26"   23"   20"

Ranges of individual timpani.

Grace Note

The timpani is primarily an orchestral or concert-band instrument, but marching bands and drum corps that have a percussion pit also make use of the instrument. In addition, you can sometimes find timpani used in some popular music, typically for isolated effects.

How many drums does a timpanist play? Small or budget-constricted ensembles (think the average junior high school concert band) might have just two drums, but most professional timpanists play four or five drums.

In a four-drum array, the drums have diameters of 32, 29, 26, and 23 inches. If you add a fifth drum to your arsenal, it's probably a *piccolo timpani*, with a diameter of 20 inches. For a two-drum setup, you typically go with the drums in the middle—the 29- and 26-inch drums.

Whether you're playing two, four, or five timpani, the drums are normally arranged in order with the largest drum on the left and the smallest on the right. This is called the French setup; the competing German setup, somewhat less popular, arranges the drums large to small from right to left. The drums have overlapping ranges, with each drum tuned to a different pitch, enabling you to play multiple notes over the course of a piece.

A five-timpani setup—the one on the far right is the piccolo timpani.

(Photo courtesy of Ludwig/Musser Percussion.)

History of the Timpani

The instrument we call timpani (or, in some instances, *tympani*) has evolved substantially over the years. While timpani are among the largest drums today, the earliest timpani were quite small. These first timpani—actually, the *kettledrums* of the twelfth and thirteenth centuries—were only about 8 inches in diameter, small enough to be attached to a player's belt as he marched along with the army. These were fixed-pitch drums, with the head nailed into the drum's shell.

By the fifteenth century, kettledrums had gotten so large that they had to be carried on horseback. They also became tunable, thanks to the addition of a counterhoop that was tied to the shell; the attaching rope was tightened or loosened to raise or lower the drum's pitch. This tuning apparatus was replaced by tensioning screws in the sixteenth century, thus enabling definite pitch tuning.

The first known orchestral work for timpani was Jean-Baptiste Lully's 1675 opera, *Thérése*. Other composers, including Bach and Handel, soon followed suit. In most of these early works, the timpani were almost always tuned with the tonic of the piece on the high drum and the dominant on the low drum—a fourth apart from bottom to top. So, for example, if a piece were in the key of C major, the timpani would be tuned to the notes G (low drum) and C (high drum).

Writing for timpani took a dramatic turn during the early 1800s. Ludwig van Beethoven gave prominence to the timpani as an independent voice, as opposed to the two-note supporting position common during the Baroque and early Classical period. Beethoven wrote for timpani tuned to intervals other than the fourth or fifth, often creating dramatic parts for the deep-voiced drums. Other composers, such as Berlioz, began to specify specific types of mallets (wooden, felt-covered, and so on) to be used in different works.

In spite of Beethoven's innovations, more sophisticated timpani parts weren't possible, due to the tuning limitations of the drums. Early timpani were tunable to specific pitches, but the drums were difficult to tune during a performance. This is because the instruments were hand-tuned, using multiple T-shaped tuning rods; all the rods had to be turned in sequence to change the pitch. This wasn't something that could be done quickly or easily.

> **Grace Note**
>
> Technically, the word *timpani* is plural, and a single drum is called a *timpano*. That said, *timpani* can be both singular or plural in common parlance.

Baroque-era timpani with individual tuning rods.

(Photo courtesy of Adams Musical Instruments/Pearl Drums.)

This changed during the 1870s, when the first pedal timpani were introduced. These so-called *Dresden timpani* (after the city where the innovation first originated) enabled precise tuning via means of a foot pedal; moving the pedal up or down activated a mechanism that tightened or loosened the top head. This innovation led the way for timpani parts that incorporated multiple pitch changes for each drum over the course of a piece.

Deconstructing the Modern Timpani

Today's timpanist plays four or five drums together, ranging from 32 to 20 inches in diameter. Regardless of the size, all modern timpani have a similar construction.

The Head

The part of the timpani you hit with the timpani mallets is the *head*. Timpani heads are typically single-ply heads, and can be made of plastic or calfskin.

Plastic heads can take considerable abuse and hold up better under temperature and humidity changes, which makes them the preferred choice for inexperienced or student players. For that matter, many experienced players prefer the ease of use afforded by plastic heads. That said, many traditionalists prefer the slightly warmer sound of calfskin heads, even if they're more temperamental.

The head is attached to the bowl by means of tensioning rods attached to a counterhoop. While older timpani had T-shaped handles for tensioning, most modern timpani put the tops of the tensioning rods flush with the head, so they don't get in the way of playing. This requires a separate tuning key, like the kind used with snare drums, to adjust the lugs.

The Bowl

The head fits on top of the timpani bowl, which amplifies the sound of the head and provides necessary resonance. The bigger the bowl, the deeper the drum's sound.

Timpani today typically have either copper or fiberglass bowls. Traditionalists prefer copper bowls, even though fiberglass can take more physical abuse without denting. (Fiberglass timpani are also much lighter, which make them ideal for traveling players.)

The Pedal

Modern timpani are tuned via means of a foot pedal. Although you still initially have to tension the head via the standard tuning rods, you change the pitch via the pedal.

The pedal tuning mechanism on a modern timpani.

(Photo courtesy of Adams Musical Instruments/Pearl Drums.)

The pedal mechanism is attached to rods that also attach to the counterhoop. To raise the drum's pitch, press the pedal down; this pulls the counterhoop down and tightens the tension of the drum's head. To lower the pitch, lift on the pedal; this releases the tension on the head.

Grace Note

Some traditionalists prefer hand-tuned timpani over pedal-tuned models. Modern hand-tuned timpani—called *chain timpani*—use a single T-shaped master tuning handle that is attached via a chain to the other tuning rods. Turning this single handle, then, turns all the other tuning rods and thus changes the pitch of the drum. Some consider this method of tuning to be more precise than pedal tuning, although it takes more time and more skill to hit the right pitch.

Tuning the Timpani

Now you know how the pedal mechanism works. But how do you tune the timpani?

First, understand that you can't immediately shift to a new pitch; tuning the drum takes a few seconds, even more if you're an experienced player. Experienced timpanists can approximate where the right pitch should be, but still need to fine-tune the pitch with incremental changes to the pedal tensioning. In this regard, tuning timpani is no different from tuning any other instrument—it's a trial-and-error process.

The most common approach to tuning the timpani to a precise pitch is called *interval tuning*. In this approach, you start by using a tuning fork, pitch pipe, or electronic tuner to tune the drum to a starter pitch—typically A (when using a tuning fork) or the first pitch in a given piece. Then, when you need to change the pitch of that drum, you hum or sing or just internalize the given interval to the next pitch and tune the drum accordingly.

Grace Note

Learn more about pitch and intervals in my companion book, *The Complete Idiot's Guide to Music Theory, Second Edition* (Alpha Books, 2005).

For example, you might use the pitch pipe to tune the drum initially to an A. If the next piece you play requires the drum to be tuned to a C, you would hum a minor third (the interval from A to C) and tune the drum to the C.

This approach requires you to develop a sense of relative pitch—knowing how to get from one pitch to another. That means learning all your intervals, from the minor second to the major seventh.

In addition, you need to be able to tune the timpani while other instruments are playing, because many pieces require pitch changes within a piece. To return to the previous example, if you are retuning from A to C, you may need to do so within a few measures in the middle of a piece. Tricky business, that.

To help with the tuning, some timpani are equipped with tuning gauges. It's important to note that these gauges are not precise indications of tuning, but rather help you get into the ballpark. So, for example, if you need to tune to an A, you can depress the pedal until the gauge reads "A," but the drum's pitch might not be precisely in tune with what the rest of the band or orchestra is playing. That is, you still may have to do fine-tuning by ear.

That said, these tuning gauges do make life easier for the working timpanist. It's better to have them than not.

Pro Tip
Show drummers in the pit of a musical often play multiple percussion instruments in addition to the timpani. When you're moving from another instrument to the timpani in a matter of beats, a tuning gauge is essential; you just don't have the time to listen to and tune the drums in the traditional fashion.

Choosing the Right Mallets

Timpani are played with felt-headed mallets, which are available in a variety of hardnesses. The felt is typically wrapped around a wood core, although felt and cork cores are also common. A softer mallet produces a more muffled sound, where harder mallets provide a more distinct attack. It's not uncommon for a timpanist to come armed with several pairs of mallets, and to change mallets according to the needs of the piece.

Good-quality mallets can have either wooden or metal handles. Metal-handled mallets typically have rubber grips; wood-handled mallets are usually naked wood. The wood used in these mallets can be hickory, maple, cherry, birch, or even bamboo. Metal mallets are constructed of either aluminum or carbon fiber.

Pro Tip
For rolls and legato passages, use softer mallets. For shorter notes and staccato passages, use harder mallets. That said, you're often required to play rolls and staccato notes in close proximity and don't have time to switch mallets; instead, you have to adjust your playing technique accordingly.

A selection of timpani mallets.

(Photo courtesy of Ludwig/Muller Percussion.)

Playing the Timpani

The timpani are arranged in an arc around the performer, with the largest drum on your left and the smallest on the right. All drums need to be in easy striking range with your mallets; the pedals also need to be within easy range of either foot.

Gripping the Mallets

Timpanists today employ either the French or German grip. Either grip is acceptable.

To play *French grip*, reach out with your hand and grab the mallet near the end so that the very end of the mallet is within the curve of your hand. Grab the handle with your thumb and the first joint of your index finger, then close your other fingers loosely around the handle. Now turn your wrist so that your thumb is on top of the mallet and your hand is close to perpendicular with the timpani head. Use the same grip with both hands.

German grip is similar to the matched grip used in snare drum and drum set playing. To play German grip, you start out the same way as with French grip, by grabbing the mallet near the end with your thumb and the first joint of your index finger. Close your other fingers around the handle, then turn your wrist so that your thumb is on the side of the handle and the mallet is perpendicular with the head. Use the same grip with both hands.

With either grip, the primary support for the mallet is provided by your thumb and index finger. Your other fingers touch the mallet only loosely.

Timpani mallets held with French grip.

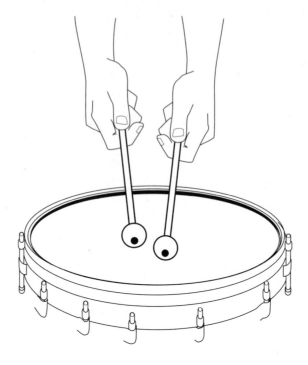

Timpani mallets held with German grip.

Striking the Drum

The timpani head is big—where do you strike it? The proper beating spot should be between the two tuning screws closest to you. Strike directly above a tuning screw and the sound is deadened.

You should strike the timpani about 3 to 4 inches in from the rim, or slightly farther in with larger drums. Striking in this area will produce the round, resonant sound you expect. If you play closer to the edge, you get a thinner sound; if you play closer to the middle, the sound becomes more muffled.

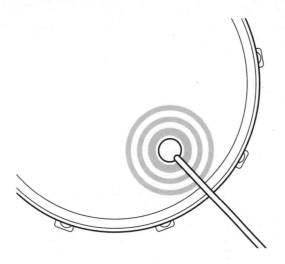

The proper beating spot for timpani.

Position the mallets close to parallel with each other, or perhaps at a small angle. Unlike the technique used with most other drums, the two timpani mallets should not strike the exact same spot on the head; it's okay to place them a few inches apart in the "sweet spot" of the head.

You strike the timpani similar to how you strike a snare drum—with a glancing blow. You don't want to bury the mallet in the head; this would create a muffled tone. Instead, try to draw the sound out of the head by lifting the mallet quickly off the head after striking it. This allows the head to vibrate and provide a proper tone.

Start by positioning the head of the mallet about 8 to 10 inches above the surface of the timpani, with your hand closer to the drum; this angles the mallet upward slightly. Use your wrist and fingers to bring the mallet down quickly to the head and then sweep the mallet back into the air, using the bounce from the head to contribute to the upward energy.

You see, unlike snare drumming, where tight control of each stroke is important, bouncing the mallet off the head is acceptable timpani technique—especially when the head is tuned in the mid to upper range. This type of bounce stroke promotes relaxation and produces a full, warm sound.

Naturally, a faster stroke creates a very articulate, ringing sound. Use a slower stroke for more legato passages.

Muffling the Drum

The basic stroke elicits a ringing, resonant note from the timpani. But you don't always want a note with that type of sustain—which means learning how to muffle the drum.

There are several ways to muffle the timpani to produce more staccato notes. The most common method is to use your hands—more specifically, the pads of your fingers. Use the third, fourth, and fifth fingers of the same hand with which you're holding the mallet. Press your fingers against the head while striking the head for an immediate muffled sound; press the head shortly after striking the head to produce notes with just a little sustain.

You can also muffle the timpani with an external mute. This is a small pad, typically made of felt or leather, that you place directly onto the drum head. This produces a very dry tone with almost no resonance, and is useful when you're playing a fast passage with a lot of notes you don't want running into each other. You can vary the amount of muffling by placing the mute at different spots on the head.

Playing a Roll

A note struck on the timpani has a certain amount of sustain, but that quickly fades under the sounds of the other instruments. To effect a longer sustain, you must roll the timpani.

A timpani roll is similar to a snare drum roll, in function if not in execution. Like a snare roll, a timpani roll is a series of fast strokes that attempts to emulate the sound of a single long note. Unlike a snare roll, where you play two (or more) notes per hand, the timpani roll is a single-stroke affair—RLRLRLRL.

To play a timpani roll, you strike the right and left mallets in rapid succession over the duration of the note. The faster the roll, the more seamless it sounds—to a point. You'll need to vary the speed of the roll by the size and tension of the drum. That is, if you're playing on one of the larger, lower-pitched timpani, you should roll slightly slower than you would on one of the smaller, higher-pitched drums. It's a subtle difference, but an important one.

Like a snare drum roll, a timpani roll is notated by placing three slashes through the stem or above the head of a note. In almost all instances, a roll is played on a single drum.

Timpani rolls.

Reading the Part

Music for timpani is always written on the bass clef staff. Timpani music looks like music for any bass clef instrument, except there won't be a lot of different pitches notated, just the notes for the five (or fewer) drums in use. Also, look for special notation for rolls, muffled notes, special effects, and the like.

A typical timpani part, from Beethoven's Symphony No. 9.

Make sure you read ahead to look for any tuning changes coming up. These may or may not be notated in the music, so you may want to mark up your part to highlight these changes.

Different Techniques for Different Sounds

Modern composers are always looking for unique sounds, and one of the places they look is at the timpani. That's because there are a variety of sounds you can get from the timpani, by using some special techniques.

First, know that different types of mallets produce different sounds. A softer mallet produces a fuller sound with a rounder attack, whereas a harder mallet produces a sharper sound with a more distinct attack. For a very crisp, almost "pingy" sound, you can even use wooden mallets—although care should be taken not to damage the timpani head.

For that matter, you can create some unique effects by striking the timpani with something other than timpani mallets. Some composers have specified timpani played with snare drumsticks (creating a very loud sound); others have written the timpani to be played with hands or fingers. A variety of sounds are possible.

Heads Up

Be very, very careful when playing timpani with snare drum sticks or wooden mallets. It's almost impossible *not* to dent timpani heads when playing loudly with sticks, especially on the larger drums. Composers who write this type of passage probably aren't familiar with the intricacies of the instrument, and are just trying to get a certain sound in what they think is a creative manner; they're not aware that the instrument is so easily damaged.

Another way to vary the sound of the timpani is to strike the head outside of the normal sweet spot. For example, when you strike the timpani directly in the center of the head, you get a tone more akin to that of a concert bass drum, almost totally devoid of pitch and resonance. Striking near the rim creates a sound that is bright but not very deep.

Most works for timpani ask you to strike one drum at a time, one after the other. You can, however, play two notes at the same time, by striking two drums together, one with each mallet. This is called a *double stop*, the same as when a violin plays two strings simultaneously.

You can also play triple and quadruple stops, by holding two mallets in each hand, much like a marimba player does. This way, you can hit two drums with each hand and thus double the number of simultaneous notes you can play.

Another interesting special effect is a short glissando played on a single timpani. You achieve this effect by striking the head and then using the foot pedal to change the pitch upward or downward, as appropriate. The effect is more like a "bo-ing" than it is a true glissando, but interesting nonetheless.

The Least You Need to Know

♦ The timpani have been used in orchestral work since the late 1600s, although it was Beethoven who redefined the role of the timpani for the modern orchestra.

♦ Most timpanists play four or five separate drums, although budget-conscious organizations can get by with just two—the 29- and 26-inch drums.

♦ Each drum has a range of about a fifth, and the ranges of different drums overlap.

♦ Modern timpani are tuned to specific pitches using an adjustable foot pedal.

♦ Timpani mallets can be made of either wood or metal with a soft felt head.

♦ Use the fingers of the striking hand to muffle a note; roll between your hands to sustain a long note.

Chapter 5

Cymbals and Gongs

In This Chapter

- ◆ Understanding the cymbal
- ◆ Playing a suspended cymbal
- ◆ Working with hand cymbals
- ◆ Learning about the gong
- ◆ Discovering the antique sound of crotales

So far in this book we've talked about drums—snare drums, bass drums, timpani. Now it's time to move onto another type of percussion instrument, one without heads and shells.

The cymbal is a fun little instrument. Unlike drums, which have lots of component parts, the cymbal is an all-in-one affair. It's one piece of metal. Strike it in different ways and in different areas and you produce different sounds; you can even hit two of them together to produce a really big crash.

And what a crash! Cymbals are very loud instruments; even though they can be played softly, their unique timbre enables them to easily cut through even the loudest orchestral passages. Plus, let's face it, playing cymbals is fun, whether you're doing a roll on a suspended cymbal or warming up a gong for a really big crash. There's a lot you can do with a cymbal or two, especially in concert work.

The History of the Cymbal

The cymbal is one of the oldest percussion instruments. Evidence of shaped pieces of metal dates back to ancient Egypt, Assyria, Persia, and Greece. In fact, the word *cymbal* is derived from the Latin *cymbalum* (itself derived from the Greek word *kumbalom*), which means a small bowl—which describes the typical cymbal shape.

Grace Note _____

Two of the earliest known cymbals, 13 centimeters in diameter, were found in the tomb of Ankhhapê, a sacred Egyptian musician.

Pro Tip

For what it's worth, the hand-hammered K. Zildjians have long been thought to be better cymbals for playing jazz, due to their darker tone. The brighter-sounding machine-hammered A. Zildjians are preferred by rock and symphonic players.

Grace Note _____

Some cymbal makers eliminate the hot-forging step by stamping the cymbal from a sheet of sheet metal. The resulting sound is less complex than that of traditionally cast and forged cymbals.

More modern cymbals evolved during the early 1600s in Constantinople, when an Armenian metalsmith named Kerope established the first Turkish cymbal factory. Kerope's son Avedis discovered a method for making a special bronze alloy from 80 percent copper and 20 percent tin. Thanks to this discovery, Avedis was given the name *Zilciyan*, meaning "family of cymbalsmiths." And thus we have the origins of the original Avedis Zildjian—a name familiar to all cymbal players today.

Up until the mid-eighteenth century, cymbals were used primarily by military bands. The first notated use of cymbals in European orchestral music was in Christoph Willibald Gluck's 1764 opera, *La Rencontre imprévue*. Mozart and Haydn followed suit, both utilizing hand cymbals in military-like passages. It was Hector Berlioz, however, who expanded the use of the instrument in the mid-1800s to include the suspended cymbal.

By 1865, the Zildjian family business became known as K. Zildjian & Cie, after Kerope Zildjian II, who brought the family's cymbals to Europe and the United States. The company split in two in the late 1920s, with A. Zildjian cymbals being made in Boston and K. Zildjians continuing to be manufactured in Turkey.

The K. Zildjian cymbals were brought back into the fold of the Avedis Zildjian Company in 1968, with the single company now selling both K. and A. Zildjian models. That wasn't the last of the family drama, however, as Robert Zildjian broke from the fold in 1981 to form Sabian, Ltd. Sabian cymbals, similar in construction to traditional A. Zildjians, are currently manufactured in Canada.

Of course, not all cymbal companies come from the Zildjian lineage. Paiste cymbals, for example, were first manufactured in the early 1900s in Estonia by Michail Toomas Paiste. Manufacture was moved to Switzerland in 1957 by his son, Michail M. Paiste, where it remains to this day.

How Cymbals Are Made

For being nothing more than a big piece of metal, it's actually quite interesting how a cymbal is made. It all starts with the metal, of course, and every cymbal maker uses its own special formulations to create its cymbal alloys. Many manufacturers use different alloys for different lines of cymbals; different alloys produce different sounds.

The cymbal maker starts by casting its alloy into a "blank," or rough-shaped piece of metal. This blank is then hot-forged to form the round shape of the cymbal.

At this point, the cymbal is cold-hammered to harden the metal, then turned on a lathe to reduce the thickness of the cymbal. Then there is additional hammering to define the cymbal's sound. This final hammering can be done by machine or by hand. True hand-hammered cymbals tend to have a darker and richer tone than machine-hammered models—and with greater variation from cymbal to cymbal. Machine-hammered cymbals tend to be brighter with a more cutting sound.

Hand hammering a cymbal.

(Photo courtesy of Paiste Cymbals.)

Other factors also help to determine a cymbal's sound. A larger cymbal tends to be "slower" with a longer sustain and deeper sound, more suitable for single notes and "ride" work. A smaller cymbal tends to have a faster response with a shorter sustain, more suitable for short crashes.

The thickness of the cymbal also affects the sound. A thicker cymbal has a darker sound and slower response, while a thinner cymbal has a brighter sound and faster response. Different cymbal alloys can also produce different tonal qualities, as can the overall shape of the cymbal, size of the bell, and so on.

In short, if you want more of a crash cymbal, go with a smaller, thinner model—something 18 inches or smaller (and the smaller the diameter, the faster the response). If you want more of a ride cymbal, go with a larger, thicker model—something 20 inches or larger.

The Parts of a Cymbal

All cymbals are round, with a taper down from the center to the edge. The center of the cymbal is called the *bell*, and contains a small hole used to attach the cymbal to a stand or to feed through straps for hand use. The sound of the bell when struck is brighter and more piercing than that of the rest of the cymbal.

The *bow* of the cymbal reaches from the bell to the edge. You strike a suspended cymbal on the bow to play individual notes; where on the bow you strike determines the sound you create.

The *edge* of the cymbal is just that: the outer edge. You hit a suspended cymbal on the edge to create a "crash" sound; striking on the edge produces a louder sound with more sustain than striking on the bow. In addition, you play rolls by striking the cymbal with mallets near the cymbal's edge.

The parts of a cymbal.

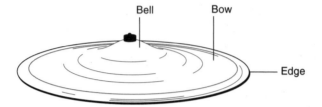

Rolling and Riding: Suspended Cymbals

There are two ways that cymbals are employed for concert and orchestral use. A single cymbal can be mounted on a stand and struck with a stick or mallet, or two cymbals can be held by hand and crashed together. We'll look at suspended cymbals first.

Suspending the Cymbal

A suspended cymbal doesn't have to be literally suspended; any cymbal on a traditional cymbal stand counts. A true suspended cymbal stand hangs the cymbal from a leather strap, which some traditionalists claim provides for maximum sustain. More modern stands sit the cymbal on top of a felt holder and are more practical for most uses.

Suspended cymbals for orchestral use can be of any size or weight, although thinner cymbals in the 16- to 18-inch range are most common, especially for creating smooth cymbal rolls and fast crashes. Larger, thicker cymbals are more difficult to control in concert use, although they're not uncommon. A typical orchestra will have several cymbals of different sizes and weights for players to choose from for different pieces.

A suspended cymbal for orchestral use.

(Photo courtesy of Paiste Cymbals.)

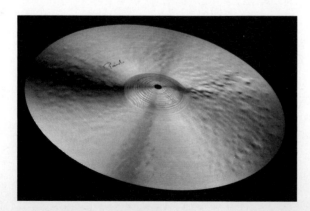

Sticks or Mallets?

You can play a suspended cymbal with sticks or with yarn- or felt-wrapped mallets, such as timpani or marimba mallets. Striking the cymbal on the bow with a stick produces a distinct "ping" sound, while striking with a soft mallet produces an indistinct "wong." (You can get an even sharper, "pingier" sound by hitting a stick—not a mallet—on the cymbal's bell.) Use sticks where distinct notes are desired; use mallets to produce a softer sound or cymbal roll.

Sticks are also necessary when you want to crash a suspended cymbal; use the butt end of the stick for best effect. While you can hit the cymbal hard enough with a mallet to produce a crash sound, the crash is muddier and often a little slow compared to the quick and sharp crash created by striking the edge of the cymbal with a stick—although the resulting sound is a lot warmer than what you get with a stick.

Pro Tip

You can create interesting effects by striking the cymbal with different types of items and in different ways. For example, scraping a coin or triangle beater down the bow of the cymbal creates a unique "zing" sound. To create an eerie, squealing sound, draw a cello bow across the edge of the cymbal.

Playing a Cymbal Roll

One of the most common uses of the suspended cymbal in orchestral work is to play a cymbal roll. Rolls can softly underscore a passage, or crescendo from soft to loud to accentuate a climax.

You play a cymbal roll with two soft mallets. Moderately soft yarn marimba mallets work best; timpani mallets are too soft (plus you'll end up destroying the felt), and hard rubber marimba mallets produce too distinct a sound when they strike the cymbal surface.

Position the mallets on the right and left opposite edges of the cymbal. Alternately, you can position the mallets close together on the edge of the cymbal nearest to you. Either approach is valid.

A cymbal roll is a single-stroke roll, RLRLRLRL. Play rapidly enough to create a continuous sound, but not so rapidly that one stroke interferes with the sustain from the previous stroke. In general, the thinner the cymbal, the slower the roll. That's because both thinner cymbals have more sustain. Roll faster on thicker cymbals.

If the piece calls for a crescendo over the course of the roll, you may want to increase the speed of the roll as you increase the volume. This helps to build up to a big climax—typically an accented crash on the final note.

Heads Up

A common mistake among inexperienced players is to position the mallets inward on the bow of the cymbal, closer to the bell. This approach produces too much audible attack from the mallets rather than a clean cymbal sustain.

Cymbal Notation

Music for cymbals varies from arranger to arranger. Technically, cymbals should be written with alternative note heads (×'s and ○'s) on a single-line percussion staff, but good luck finding that. More often, you'll find cymbal parts with standard note heads on a five-line percussion or treble clef staff. In either case, the length of the note is the length of the note.

A cymbal part written with alternative notation—the final note should be a crash.

The disadvantage of using standard note heads is that you don't know when you should ride and when you should crash the cymbal, unless it's noted in text beside the note. A good rule of thumb is that if it's a short unaccented note, you play a single "ping." If it's a long, accented note, it's probably a crash.

Reading is easier with alternative notation. If the note head is an ×, it's a short "ping." If it's an open ○, it's a crash. In either type of notation, a roll is a roll and is notated with either three slash marks or a trill mark, as in the following example. If the main note ties to a second, ending note, the roll should end with a crash. If not, the roll just tapers off at the end of the note.

The suspended cymbal part from the end of Claude Debussy's La Mer—*a continuous crescendo roll.*

The Big Crash: Hand Cymbals

 Suspended cymbals aren't the only cymbals used in orchestral work. Hand cymbals—two cymbals held in your hands and struck together—are used to provide different effects, including loud crashes.

A pair of orchestral hand cymbals.

(Photo courtesy of Paiste Cymbals.)

Choosing Hand Cymbals

Hand cymbals come in all manner of sizes and weights, from 16-inch light to 20-inch heavy. The larger the cymbal, the louder the sound and the longer the sustain. That said, smaller cymbals are easier to control (they're a lot lighter to hold, too) and are better for short bursts of sound.

You hold hand cymbals with leather straps that feed through the cymbal's center hole. You can put your hand through the strap or not; that's the player's prerogative—although most orchestral players grab the straps from the outside, which is quicker. Just grab the inner edge of the strap between your thumb and fingers and hold on tight.

Heads Up
Sometimes you'll see the strap of a hand cymbal fed through a pad that keeps your hand from touching the cymbal during use. While these pads are somewhat common in marching band use, where they help reduce hand fatigue, they're not typically recommended for orchestral work, as they diminish the resonance of the cymbals.

Different Techniques

The most common use of hand cymbals is to create a crash sound. This is accomplished by striking one cymbal into the other, or both into each other. Start with the cymbals about 6 inches apart, one slightly above the other, then raise and lower your arms to slap the cymbals together.

Grace Note
Hand cymbals are sometimes called *crash cymbals,* even though they can do more than just crash. Don't confuse orchestral or marching crash cymbals with similarly named crash cymbals on a drum set; the latter cymbals are single cymbals with a single purpose only.

You don't want to crash the cymbals head on, however; strike the cymbals at a slight angle to each other for best effect. The cymbals should come together in the crash and then move apart, each sustaining on its own. You want the edges of the two cymbals to hit against each other but not hold together. To create a louder crash, start with more of a backstroke and strike the cymbals harder. Follow through with both your arms moving in the direction of each stroke—keep the cymbals perpendicular to your body, don't turn them outward to the audience.

Heads Up
If you force the two cymbals together straight on, the edges meet directly and don't allow sufficient vibration for an acceptable sustain. Instead, start with one cymbal higher than the other and strike them together with one arm moving down and the other moving up.

The length of the crash should correspond to the length of the written note, with some interpretation allowed. For example, if it's a big, accented crash, you may want to let the sustain extend past the note as written. To end the sustain, press the cymbals close against your body.

Playing a full crash with hand cymbals.

Not all crashes are big, accented affairs. Some works call for a series of short, unaccented crashes, often accompanying the bass drum note for note. This type of crash is created by softly clashing the cymbals together from a short distance apart. Successive clashes are created using a short up-down motion between your two hands.

You can create a "chick" effect by forcing the two cymbals together from a short distance apart. Unlike a crash, where the cymbals move together and then apart, the "chick" is created when the two cymbals come together and stay together. No crash is involved.

Pro Tip

To shorten or muffle the notes you play, pull the two cymbals into your stomach immediately after the crash.

Welcome to the Gong Show

Gongs come to us from the Malay-Javanese region and have been used in almost all Asian cultures. In modern times, the gong has become a fixture in the concert band and orchestra, although used sparingly.

 Grace Note _____

Technically, a gong is an instrument that has a raised center section or "nipple," and produces a specific pitch. The instrument most of us call a gong is actually a *tam-tam;* the tam-tam lacks the center nipple and produces an indefinite pitch. In everyday usage, however, tam-tams are called gongs and that's probably what you'll be playing.

Getting to Know the Gong

A gong is a round disc of metal like a cymbal, but thicker and with an in-turned edge. The bell is also less pronounced, and there's less of an angle from the bell across the bow.

A symphonic gong.

(Photo courtesy of Paiste Cymbals.)

And then there's the sound. A gong doesn't really sound like a cymbal. The sound is larger and "whoosier," starting soft and expanding into a loud "whaaaw" with a long sustain and complex overtones. You can strike individual notes or even create an impressive roll.

Gongs for orchestral use typically range from 24 to 38 inches in diameter, although larger gongs (up to 80 inches!) exist. Smaller gongs, in the 10-inch range, are used for special effects and are less common.

Choosing Mallets

You don't play a symphonic gong with sticks or marimba mallets. Instead, you use special gong mallets with soft heads covered in yarn, wool, or felt. The larger the gong, the larger the mallet.

Most orchestral pieces call for a single mallet to strike single long notes. When the rare gong roll is notated, two mallets are required.

A gong mallet.

(Photo courtesy of Pro-Mark.)

Playing the Gong

Because of its large size, you just can't strike a gong "cold." It takes a little warming up—that is, a pre-vibration—for the gong to achieve its desired sound.

This warming up of a gong is called *priming*. To prime a gong, you lightly strike around the edge of the gong with the mallet, soft enough not to make a noticeable sound but hard enough to get the surface vibrating. Priming might take several seconds; when the gong is sufficiently primed, you can then strike it as required.

You strike the gong with an indirect stroke, at an angle about 45 degrees to the surface. This produces the best balance of attack and sustain; striking more directly (at a 90-degree angle) produces a louder but more percussive tone.

As to where you strike the gong, that depends on the sound you want. Striking near the edge creates a lighter sound, while striking toward the center creates a louder, deeper tone. The best sound for most orchestral work is achieved by striking the gong just below the center.

Strike near the edge for a lighter sound, or closer to the center for a deeper tone.

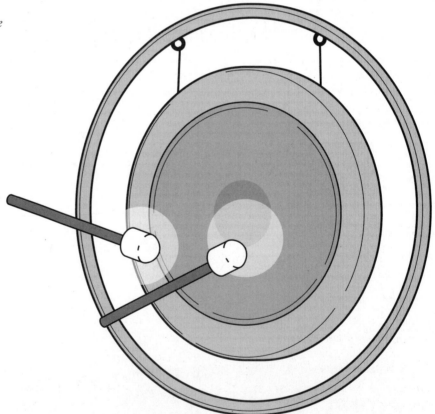

You roll on a gong similar to the way you roll on a cymbal. Use two mallets positioned on opposite sides of the gong, toward the edges. The speed of your roll should be relatively slow, given the size of the instrument. Be careful not to let the sound get away from you, as successive strikes continue to build harmonics and sustain—often to an uncontrollable point!

To muffle the gong, use any and all parts of your body. Press your arms and legs against the instrument, or even hug it to your midsection. The larger the gong, the more difficult it will be to mute in this fashion.

Heads Up

You don't want to strike the gong in the exact center, as the tone will be somewhat muffled—and, if you strike it hard enough, you could break the gong!

Antique Cymbals: Crotales

The final concert cymbal we'll discuss is actually a pitched percussion instrument, like the xylophone or glockenspiel. The *crotale* (pronounced "kro-TAH-lee"), also known as an *antique cymbal*, is a small (4 inches or so) metal disk tuned to a specific pitch. You typically find crotales in one- or two-octave sets.

You play crotales like you do the glockenspiel, with hard plastic or brass mallets. For the fullest sound, strike the crotale near the instrument's edge; play closer to the bell to produce a noticeably thinner sound. Played properly, the sound is like a small bell, clear and piercing.

Because they're pitched instruments, playing crotales is a little like playing a mallet percussion instrument. Notation is for specific pitches, written on the treble clef staff. They sound two octaves higher than written.

Grace Note

We'll discuss one other type of cymbal later in this book. *Finger cymbals* are very small non-pitched cymbals from the Middle East, as discussed in Chapter 14.

An octave's worth of crotales.

(Photo courtesy of Sabian Cymbals.)

The Least You Need to Know

◆ Cymbals are available in all different sizes, weights, and designs.

◆ Suspended cymbals are used in orchestral work for riding, crashing, and rolling.

◆ Hand cymbals are used primarily for crashes, but also can create other effects.

◆ When a big sound is called for, use a big gong—but make sure you prime it first!

◆ Crotales are small, definite pitched cymbals with a piercing bell-like sound.

Chapter 6

Mallets, Bells, and Chimes

In This Chapter

- Choosing the best mallets for your instrument
- Learning how to play melodic percussion instruments—with one, two, or four mallets
- Understanding the marimba, xylophone, and vibraphone
- Getting to know the glockenspiel and chimes

Up until now, we've discussed percussion instruments that are mainly used for rhythm—things that go *bang* or *crash* when you hit them. But there are other percussion instruments that sound specific pitches when you hit them, and they're used to play melodies and harmonies, just like string and wind instruments.

The melodic instruments of the percussion family all have multiple bars or tubes arranged like a piano keyboard. These instruments—the marimba, xylophone, bells, and chimes—give melodic voice to the percussion section.

Understanding Melodic Percussion

We'll call these pitched percussion instruments *melodic percussion*, to distinguish them from pitched drums (such as the timpani and Roto Toms) that really aren't used to play melodies. Marimbas and xylophones and such *are* used to play melodies, either singularly or in concert with other instruments of the orchestra.

All melodic percussion instruments are similar in construction. The instrument is made from a series of wooden, synthetic, or metal bars. Each bar is tuned to a specific pitch—E♭, for example, or A. The bars are arranged like the keys on a piano keyboard, with the "white" notes on one level and the "black" notes (the flats and sharps) above that. The bars, obviously, are arranged from lowest on the left to highest on the right.

The first melodic percussion instruments evolved independently on the west coast of Africa, Asia, and Indonesia, with the earliest known instrument dating to 2000 B.C.E. in China. The African instruments, such as the *gyil*, are similar to modern-day xylophones but with only a dozen or so bars, tuned to a pentatonic scale rather than the Western chromatic scale. Asian and Indonesian melodic percussion, such as the Indonesian *gambang*, have more bars and thus a wider range.

Melodic percussion instruments traveled to Europe during the Crusades. The xylophone was the first such instrument to gain popularity in Western music, entering written music during the sixteenth century. By the nineteenth century, the xylophone became popular in eastern European folk music, and entered classical repertoire soon after.

Of all the various melodic percussion instruments, the marimba has the largest range and the glockenspiel the smallest. Some instruments use *resonators* below each bar to amplify the sound acoustically and help it resonate longer. Some use a pedal mechanism to dampen the bars' sustain.

Most melodic percussion instruments have horizontal keyboards—that is, the bars are arranged on a plane that is parallel with the floor, and you play them from above. Some melodic instruments, however—such as the chimes—have keyboards that are perpendicular to the floor, and the musician stands beside them when playing them.

The melodic percussion instruments cover a wide range of notes, from the bottom note of the marimba to the top note of the glockenspiel. While individual instruments may differ slightly, the following table outlines the typical range for each instrument.

> **Grace Note**
>
> The top row of notes on a melodic percussion instrument is called the *upper manual*; the lower notes (corresponding to the white notes on a piano keyboard) are called the *lower manual*.

> **def•i•ni•tion**
>
> **8va** means that the note sounds one octave higher than written.

Ranges of Mallet Percussion Instruments

Instrument	Typical Range (concert pitch)
Marimba	
Xylophone	

Instrument	Typical Range (concert pitch)
Vibraphone	
Glockenspiel	
Chimes	

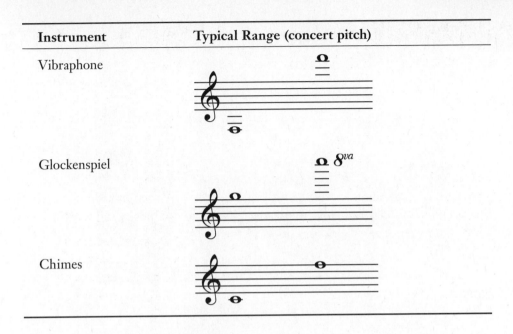

Choosing the Right Mallets

All melodic percussion instruments are played with mallets of various sorts, which is why they're sometimes referred to as *mallet instruments*. Different instruments—and different sounds—require different types of mallets.

Most mallets have a similar construction, with a shaft (handle) and a head. The exception is the chime mallet, which looks like a small wooden hammer.

The shaft can be made of wood (typically rattan or birch) or fiberglass, and is typically quite thin. Wooden shafts have more give than fiberglass ones, with rattan being the most flexible.

The mallet head can be made from any type of material. The hardest heads are made from metal or plastic and produce a hard sound when struck. Rubber mallets are softer, and produce a "clink" when struck against the instrument's bars. Yarn-wrapped or cord-wrapped mallets are softer yet and produce a less distinct, more muted sound.

In general, the higher-pitched the instrument, the harder the mallet. So, for example, the high-pitched glockenspiel is typically struck with metal or plastic mallets, while the lower-pitched marimba is struck with soft rubber or yarn-covered mallets. The next table details which types of mallets are used with which instruments.

A brass-headed mallet, for use with the glockenspiel.

(Photo courtesy of Pro-Mark.)

A selection of hard plastic mallets, ideal for glockenspiel and xylophone work.

(Photo courtesy of Ludwig/Musser Percussion.)

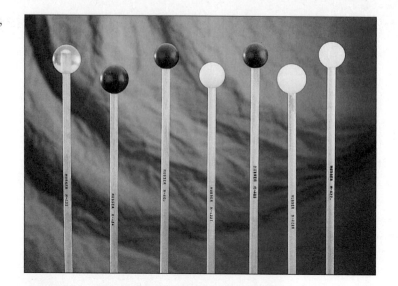

A selection of rubber mallets of various levels of hardness.

(Photo courtesy of Ludwig/Musser Percussion.)

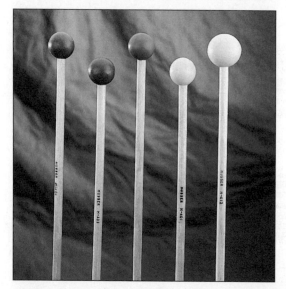

A selection of yarn-covered mallets, ideal for playing marimbas.

(Photo courtesy of Ludwig/Musser Percussion.)

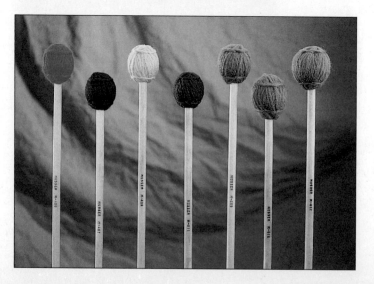

> ### Pro Tip
> While yarn-wrapped mallets are ideal for use with marimbas, they're sometimes too soft for vibes—they don't produce a clear attack. For vibraphone playing, then, cord-wrapped mallets are often preferred.

Mallets for Melodic Percussion Instruments

	Glockenspiel	Xylophone	Marimba	Vibraphone
Metal (hard)	Yes			
Plastic (hard)	Yes	Yes		
Rubber (medium)	Yes	Yes	Yes	
Cotton cord (medium)			Yes	Yes
Yarn (medium-soft)			Yes	Yes

Not all mallets of a given type are of the same hardness, however. Some yarn mallets, for example, are harder than others. The harder the mallet, the sharper the sound; the softer the mallet, the less noticeable the attack—and the more prominent the underlying pitch.

> ### Pro Tip
> Most players carry several types of mallets to use in different playing situations.

Playing Melodic Percussion

Chimes being the notable exception, most melodic percussion instruments are played in a similar fashion. The instrument is typically played with two mallets, one in each hand—although four-mallet technique is popular on both marimba and vibes. You approach the instrument as you would a piano keyboard, and play either single-line melodies or multiple-note chords.

Holding the Mallets

You can use a number of different grips when playing melodic percussion instruments. For two-mallet playing (one in each hand), both the French and German grips are popular. As you recall from Chapter 5, these grips are similar to the snare drum matched grip: You hold the mallet between the thumb and first finger, with the thumb either on top (French) or on the side (German) of the mallet.

Whichever grip you use, grasp the mallet near the end so that the butt end rests within your palm. While the stroke is generated from the wrist, movement is controlled with the last three fingers of your hand, using the thumb and index finger as a fulcrum. When playing on the same bar, the two mallets should form close to a 45-degree angle.

Playing with Four Mallets

Much marimba and vibraphone music is written for four mallets—two in each hand. This lets you play full four-note chords on the instrument. (Melodic lines are still played one note at a time, using just one of the two mallets in each hand.)

There are three primary types of grips for four-mallet playing: traditional, Burton, and Musser/Stevens. Each has its own pros and cons; none is "preferred" over the others, and each is popular in its own way.

For example, some players feel it's easier to hold a constant interval between the two mallets with the Burton grip. Others feel it's easier to do quick interval changes—to change the spacing between the mallets—with the Musser/Stevens grip. The reality is that you can play the same notes with any grip; you just have to practice.

Traditional Grip

We'll start with what's called the *traditional grip*. This four-mallet grip is called traditional because it's the oldest of the four current grips, dating in use back to around 1900. It's also the grip that's easiest to grasp, at least for beginners.

With the traditional grip, the two mallets are held one over the other in a cross at the back of the palm, with the outside mallet underneath. The thumb and first finger go between the two mallets and are used to lever the mallets apart for a larger interval. The third and fourth fingers hold the interval in place and, with the aid of the thumb, push the mallets together for a smaller interval.

Pro Tip

When playing a linear melodic line with a four-mallet grip, use the two inside mallets only.

Grace Note

Because the mallets cross over each other in your palm, some players refer to the traditional grip as the *cross grip*.

The traditional grip for four-mallet playing.

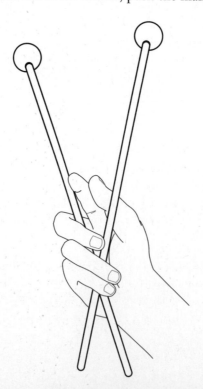

The primary advantage of the traditional grip is how easy it is to learn. The primary disadvantage is that it ties the two mallets together more than with the other grips—that is, there's less independence between the mallets. This also results in a weaker hold on each mallet. In addition, it's more difficult to reach large intervals with the traditional grip, which makes it less than ideal for marimba use.

Burton Grip

The *Burton grip* was developed by jazz vibraphonist Gary Burton in the 1960s. It's a variant of the cross grip, but functions in a much different manner.

This grip starts with the outside mallet crossed over the inside mallet. The end of the inside mallet is held with the little finger, while the outside mallet is held between the index finger and middle finger. The thumb is typically placed inside the inside mallet, but can also be placed between the two mallets to widen the interval.

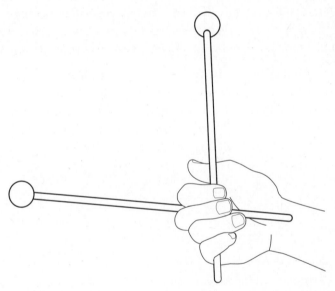

The Burton grip for four-mallet playing.

You widen the interval by pulling the end of the inside mallet away from the palm using the third and fourth fingers. You close the interval by pushing the inside mallet toward the palm, using the same fingers but with the assistance of the thumb and forefinger. The middle finger holds the outside mallet in place.

The Burton grip provides a slightly stronger grip on each mallet than does the traditional grip, which lets you achieve louder volume than with other grips—especially when playing block chords. As with the traditional grip, you don't quite get the reach to do large intervals on the marimba, which has wider bars than the vibraphone.

Grace Note

Probably because the Burton grip was created by a vibes player, it's seldom used on the marimba—making it an almost-exclusive vibraphone grip.

Musser/Stevens Grip

The *Musser/Stevens grip* is probably the most-used four-mallet grip in orchestral work. It's based on a grip developed during the 1920s by Clair Omar Musser, a legendary marimba player (and the founder of the company that still bears his name) and refined by marimba virtuoso Leigh Howard Stevens when he was a student at the Eastman School of Music in the early 1970s.

This grip is a non-crossing grip—that is, the mallets do not cross in your hand. Instead, each mallet is held separately by a different set of fingers. The outside mallet is held by the third and fourth fingers, while the inside mallet is held by the thumb, first finger, and second finger.

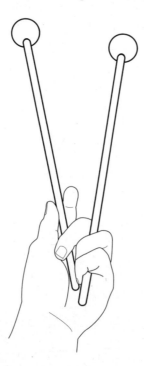

The Musser/Stevens grip for four-mallet playing.

In the basic Musser grip, you increase the interval between the mallets by pushing the thumb and first finger out and to the side, which pivots the inside mallet around a point on your palm. You decrease the interval by pulling the thumb and first finger back in, pivoting the inside mallet to the inside.

The Stevens variation on the basic Musser grip—what Stevens himself referred to as the "modified Musser grip"—concerns the pivot point. Compared to the plain Musser grip, the inside mallet pivots around a curved line in the palm rather than a fixed point. You increase the interval between the mallets by rotating the inside mallet up and out with the thumb, first finger, and second finger, along a smooth, curved line. The weight of the inside mallet transfers from the first to the second finger as the interval spreads. You decrease the interval by using the same fingers to pull the inside mallet down and in along the same curve.

While the Musser/Stevens grip is more difficult to learn than either the traditional or Burton grips, it does offer some advantages. First, it allows a stronger grip on each mallet, which makes it better for performing louder passages. In addition, you get a slightly wider space between the two mallets, which makes it easier to play larger intervals on the marimba. For these reasons, this grip is one of the most popular grips used today, especially for marimba work.

Striking the Bars

You play all horizontal melodic instruments, as well as the glockenspiel, by striking near the middle of each bar. If you can't reach the middle (as sometimes happens when playing a large interval with four mallets), you can strike the edge of the bar for a similar tone. It's most common to strike the edge of the bars on the upper manual (the black keys on a piano keyboard), not the lower.

Strike the bar with a rapid up-and-down movement, as near perpendicular as the passage allows. Make sure to pull the mallet off the bar rather than burying it in the bar. You want to give the bar full facility to resonate.

Playing a Roll

One technique common to all melodic percussion instruments is the roll. You can roll with two mallets (one in each hand) on a single note, two mallets on two different notes, and four mallets on four different notes.

A roll is notated by placing three slashes through the stem of a note, or above or below a whole note. If you're rolling on multiple notes—essentially creating a chord—the individual notes of the chord are stacked one on top of another. Position your mallets from left to right on the notes from lowest to highest.

Pro Tip
Sometimes it's more efficient to stagger the mallets when playing four-note chords— that is, to have the top mallet of the left hand play a higher note than the lower mallet of the right hand. For example, a chord consisting of the notes C, C#, F, and F# is difficult to play in traditional top-to-bottom order; a better positioning is to play the C and F with one hand and the C# and F# with the other hand, positioned above them.

One-, two-, and four-note mallet rolls.

A two-mallet roll is accomplished by hitting the right and left mallets in rapid succession over the duration of the note, like this: RLRLRLRL. The faster the roll, the more seamless it should sound; the goal is to emulate the type of single-note sustain possible on wind or string instruments.

If you're playing a single-note roll, the two mallets should hit the same bar in the same spot, one after another—although logistics may dictate playing one mallet in the center of the bar and the other on the edge. If you're playing a two-note roll, the two mallets hit two different bars.

A four-mallet roll is a slightly different beast. For example, do you hit the two mallets in each hand simultaneously, doing a stacked RLRLRL move? Or do you somehow try to achieve a distinct four-note roll, with each of the four mallets hitting separately?

The answer is that you probably want all four notes of the roll to sound individually. This requires a literal "rolling" or rippling motion between the four mallets. You turn or roll each hand so that the two mallets in that hand hit one after another. Roll from your leftmost mallet to the rightmost one, so that the notes sound lowest to highest. Starting with the bottom mallet on the left hand (call it mallet 4) and going to the top mallet on the right hand (mallet 1), the notation should look like the following:

4 3 2 1

You can also reverse this order and go from the far right to the far left, like this:

1 2 3 4

Other variations are possible, of course. One particularly good-sounding pattern looks like this:

4 3 1 2

This pattern goes from bottom-to-top with the left hand and top-to-bottom with the right. Whichever sticking you use, the point is not to strike any two notes at the same time—one note should follow the other in the roll.

Dark and Resonant: The Marimba

The marimba is the lowest-pitched keyboard percussion instrument. (We'll leave the chimes aside for the moment.) It's a large instrument, with more notes and larger bars than that of the xylophone or vibraphone.

While the marimba is evolved from the African xylophone, the modern instrument was actually developed in Central America. The first marimba with chromatic bars was made by Jose Chaequin and Manual Lopez in 1874, in Guatemala; in fact, the marimba is the national instrument of that nation.

The marimba migrated to North America in 1908 thanks to Sebastian Hurtado and his family marimba band. The instrument gained popularity after that, and soon began to be incorporated in both symphonic and popular music.

Two marimbas—one with ornamental front resonators.

(Photo courtesy of Ludwig/Musser Percussion.)

Deconstructing the Marimba

The bars of the marimba are wider than those of the xylophone, which makes for a larger instrument overall. Marimba bars are traditionally made from rosewood, although synthetic wood (such as Kelon) is used in some models. The underside of each bar is curved, which gives the instrument a very rich tone.

This tone is also affected by the use of large metal resonators beneath the bars, which help to both round off and slightly amplify the sound. The length of each resonator varies according to the pitch of the bar to which it is affixed; lower notes have bigger resonators.

You can find marimbas of various sizes, running from 4 to 5½ octaves in range. The larger instruments expand the range downward; all marimbas have the same high-C top note. Notation can be on either the treble or bass clef staffs, or on the grand staff (both bass and treble clef staffs).

> **Grace Note**
>
> For purely decorative purposes, some marimbas feature resonators for the higher notes that match the length of the resonators for the bottom notes, creating a pleasant-looking curve when viewed from the front.

Playing the Marimba

The marimba is perhaps the most versatile melodic percussion instrument, with varied colors across its entire range. In its lower registers, the marimba produces an almost mellow tone. In contrast, its top octave has a similar sound to the xylophone. Notes sustain slightly longer than with the xylophone, but still not quite as long as with the glockenspiel or vibraphone; you'll need to roll most longer notes not notated as such.

The marimba can be played with either two or four mallets, with four-mallet parts quite common in orchestral music. Yarn-covered mallets of varying degrees of hardness are most popular, but rubber mallets are also used. As with all mallet percussion instruments, softer mallets produce a rounder tone with a softer attack; harder mallets have a more distinct attack and produce a thinner tone.

As with all mallet instruments, striking in the center of the bars produces the best resonance, although striking near the edge of the bars is also good. Use two mallets to play linear passages, or four mallets to play chords. For four-mallet playing, both the traditional and Musser/Stevens grips are popular. Whichever grip you use, make sure you lift the mallets immediately after striking to let the notes "sing"; burying the mallets in the bars produces an undesirable dead tone.

A typical marimba part for two mallets.

Bright and Sunny: The Xylophone

The xylophone is the soprano voice in the keyboard percussion section, often functioning in a piccolo-like role. To untrained eyes, it looks like a miniature marimba—although its history actually predates the larger instrument.

The xylophone is thought to have originated in Southeast Asia sometime in the fourteenth century, in Indonesian Gamelan music. Believe it or not, the original xylophones were just a few wooden bars laid across the player's legs; frame-mounted bars were a later development. The instrument eventually spread to Africa and Europe, gaining favor as an eastern European folk instrument in the 1800s and getting added to the modern orchestra shortly after.

Deconstructing the Xylophone

The modern xylophone is built from a series of small wooden (rosewood) or synthetic bars. These bars, smaller than those used on the marimba, produce a very sharp, high-pitched, biting sound. Resonating tubes beneath the bars help to add a little fullness to the typically brittle sound.

Most concert xylophones have a 3½ octave range, from F to C. Smaller models narrow that range to 2½ octaves, and some larger models stretch it to 4 octaves. Compared to the marimba, the xylophone is both smaller and higher-pitched—and has a less full, less resonant tone.

A three-octave xylophone.

(Photo courtesy of Adams Musical Instruments/Pearl Drums.)

Playing the Xylophone

The xylophone is typically played with two mallets; four-mallet parts are rare to nonexistent. Harder mallets, with either plastic or hard rubber heads, produce the best attack. The instrument has no natural sustain, except in the lowest part of the range, so longer notes must be executed via rolling.

Expect to play a lot of rolls, as composers tend to favor that technique on the instrument. Rolls can be played either on one note or two notes, as a chord with one note per mallet. For a single-note roll, notation is either the traditional three slashes above the note or a trill mark. For a roll between two notes (one on each hand), the roll can be notated as a traditional stacked-note chord or with two notes side-by-side and slashes or trills between the notes.

Xylophone parts are also full of fast runs, as is common with all higher-pitched instruments. Many of these runs are either up and down the scale or up and down a chord in arpeggios. (This is a good reason to practice your 16th-note scales and arpeggios—at fast tempos!)

A typically frantic xylophone part from Stravinsky's Firebird Suite.

Plug It In—or Not: The Vibraphone

The vibraphone is a much newer instrument than the marimba or xylophone, both of which date back multiple centuries in design. The first musical instrument called *vibraphone* was introduced in 1921 by the Leedy Manufacturing Company, making it the rare percussion instrument developed in the

Grace Note

The vibraphone is also referred to as *vibes*.

United States. The sustain pedal was added in 1928 by Leedy's competitor, J. C. Deagan, Inc., which called its instrument the *vibraharp*.

Deconstructing the Vibraphone

The vibraphone looks a little like a smaller, shinier version of the marimba— with a pedal. It differs from the marimba and xylophone in that its bars are made of metal (aluminum), not wood. This produces a brighter sound than the other instruments, with more sustain.

The standard vibraphone is a three-octave instrument, starting on the F below middle C. Larger instruments, which stretch the range to four octaves (starting on the C below the F), are becoming more common, especially in orchestral work.

Using the Vibrato

One unique feature of the vibraphone is the instrument's electronic motor, which requires connection to a nearby power outlet. (It is, perhaps, the only electric percussion instrument.) This motor rotates metal plates within the instrument's resonators. The rotating plates "open" and "close" the resonators in turn, creating a pulsating type of vibrato—a "wah wah wah" type of sound.

The instrument can be played with or without the motor running; you can also vary the speed of the vibrato. With the motor off, the sound is very clear and bell-like. With the motor on, you get a distinct vibrato to all sustained notes. Vibes parts should be notated for either vibrato on or off; when in doubt, leave the motor off.

A vibraphone—keyboard percussion with a sustain pedal.

(Photo courtesy of Ludwig/ Musser Percussion.)

Working the Pedal

Unlike other keyboard percussion instruments (chimes excluded, as always), the vibraphone has a sustain pedal, like that of the piano. This enables the use of sustained notes (with or without the vibrato turned on) without rolling—although you can still roll if the music calls for it. When the pedal is up, all the bars are dampened and the sound of each note is quite short. When the pedal is depressed, the bars have full sustain.

Because of this rather long sustain, you often have to dampen individual notes as you play. You can dampen the entire keyboard, of course, by lifting the sustain pedal. Individual notes can be dampened with your hand (typically the hand you used to strike the bar) or by pressing the opposite mallet against a ringing bar.

You can also work the pedal up and down to phrase notes together in a passage. Keep the pedal down for full sustain throughout the phrase, then lift at the end to cut the ring and insert some space between that phrase and the next.

Playing the Vibraphone

Motor and sustain pedal aside, you play the vibraphone in much the same fashion as you play the marimba. Music for the vibraphone is typically notated in treble clef.

Like the marimba, the vibraphone can be played with either two or four mallets. Two-mallet technique is typically used when playing melodies only, while four mallets can be used to play both chords and linear melody notes. Both traditional and Burton grips are popular when playing with four mallets.

Vibes mallets are typically cord-wound, with various degrees of hardness. As you might expect, the harder the mallet, the more sharp and bell-like the tone; use softer mallets for more subtle accompaniment.

> **Pro Tip**
>
> Vibes are quite popular in jazz music. Many jazz vibists play the instrument like a piano, playing two-note chords with the left hand and melodies with the right.

A typical vibraphone part, for two mallets.

Bells, Bells, Bells: The Glockenspiel

The glockenspiel is the very top voice of the pitched percussion section, higher even than the xylophone. It produces a piercing, bell-like sound, which is why the instrument is sometimes called *orchestra bells*.

Deconstructing the Glockenspiel

The glockenspiel is a much smaller instrument than even the xylophone. It consists of a series of small metal bars, arranged in piano keyboard order. The concert glockenspiel is played horizontally, typically placed on a stand at about waist height.

The modern glockenspiel typically has a 2½- or 3-octave range. Notes sound two octaves higher than written.

Grace Note _____

While similar to the concert glockenspiel, the glockenspiel used in marching bands and drum and bugle corps is played vertically, held in front of the player with the lowest notes at the bottom and the highest notes at the top. Learn more in Chapter 9.

Three different types of glockenspiels.

(Photo courtesy of Ludwig/Musser Percussion.)

Playing the Glockenspiel

You play the glockenspiel with metal, plastic, or hard-rubber mallets, one in each hand. The notes ring for some time after being hit, unless dampened. You muffle a ringing note by placing your hand on the bar.

In concert band and orchestral settings, the glockenspiel is played with two mallets—never four. By using two mallets, you can effect a roll on the instrument, using the same techniques employed with other mallet percussion instruments.

That's right, even though the glockenspiel has a long natural ring, rolled notes are not uncommon. Rolls can be notated with either the traditional three slashes above the note or with a trill mark; this last method is probably most common, as many composers write similar trills for glockenspiel, flutes, and piccolos.

A typical high-reaching glockenspiel part, from Wolfgang Amadeus Mozart's The Magic Flute.

Tubular Bells: Chimes

The chimes are a unique instrument within the melodic percussion family. Instead of bars, you have tubes, and instead of a horizontal layout, everything is vertical.

Deconstructing the Chimes

A set of chimes consists of almost an octave-and-a-half's worth of long metal tubes, starting at middle C and going up from there. Each tube is tuned to a specific pitch; the tubes range from 1¼ to 1½ inches in diameter.

The chimes produce a loud ringing tone that has the same slightly out-of-tune quality as church bells. (This leads to a common use of the chimes to mimic the sound of church bells in a composition.) The instrument's sound is quite prominent within ensembles of any size; they really cut through, so musicians need to be subtle when playing them.

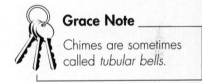

Grace Note

Chimes are sometimes called *tubular bells*.

Playing the Chimes

You play the chimes with wooden or acrylic mallets that are actually more like small hammers than marimba or xylophone mallets; some mallets have rubber heads. Strike the mallet against the top edge of the tube with the meat of the mallet, using a glancing blow. The strength of your stroke determines the dynamic level; hit harder to play louder.

Hitting harder also increases the chimes' sustain, of course. Use a softer mallet for a less distinct attack, or a harder wood or plastic-headed mallet for a "clankier" sound.

You can use either one or two mallets. Most chime parts consist of a series of longer notes, so a single mallet should suffice. For parts with more complexity, use two mallets, one in each hand.

It's important to know that chimes have considerable sustain and can ring for what seems like forever. To cut the sustain (and play shorter notes), dampen the tubes with the instrument's foot pedal—down to muffle, up for full sustain. You can also dampen the individual tubes with your hands, to create a more legato phrasing.

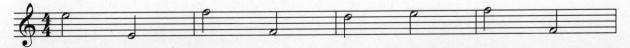

A typical part for chimes—lots of long notes.

A set of chimes.

(Photo courtesy of Adams Musical Instruments/Pearl Drums.)

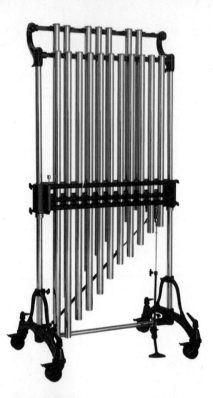

Chime mallets.

(Photo courtesy of Ludwig/Musser Percussion.)

The Least You Need to Know

- ◆ All melodic percussion instruments consist of multiple bars or tubes, each with a specific pitch, and are played like similar keyboard instruments.

- ◆ The marimba is the lowest voice of the melodic percussion family, used to play both melodies and multiple-note chords.

- ◆ The xylophone is a fun little instrument with a bright, almost brittle sound.

◆ The vibraphone has metal bars and a motor that can be used to produce a vibrato on sustained notes.

◆ The glockenspiel has a clear tone that cuts through the entire orchestra.

◆ Chimes are an octave-and-a-half worth of pitched tubes that you play with a small wooden hammer.

Auxiliary Percussion

In This Chapter

- ◆ Striking the triangle
- ◆ Shaking—and rolling—the tambourine
- ◆ Playing woodblocks and temple blocks
- ◆ Discovering other small percussion instruments

The orchestral percussionist must be well-versed on a number of different instruments—not just the big instruments, such as marimba, timpani, and snare drum that we've already discussed. The well-rounded percussionist must also be able to pick up and play a variety of smaller, more idiosyncratic instruments that may pop up in this piece or that.

What types of unusual little instruments inhabit the orchestral percussionist's toy box? We're talking relatively common instruments, such as the triangle and tambourine, as well as less common ones, such as the thundersheet and temple blocks. In fact, the more modern the music you play, the more likely you are to encounter these auxiliary percussion instruments—which means that you need to know your way around all of them.

Ding, Ding, Ding Goes the Triangle

 We'll start our trek through the auxiliary percussion jungle with an instrument you're probably familiar with: the *triangle*. It's a cute little instrument but one that's been widely used in orchestral music since the mid-1800s.

Understanding the Triangle

The triangle is a steel rod bent into the three-sided shape that gives the instrument its name. This leaves one small open end of the triangle, where the two ends of the rod almost—but don't quite—meet.

A triangle.

(Photo courtesy of Remo, Inc.)

Triangles can be of various sizes, anywhere from 4 to 10 inches in diameter. The larger the triangle, the lower pitched its sound. The triangle is hung from one of the bent corners, with a thin piece of string or wire attached to a clip of some sort. You can hold the attached clip in your hand or attach it to a music stand or other stand, which enables the triangle to vibrate freely when struck.

Playing the Triangle

You get the best tone by striking the metal triangle with a metal beater. Use a lighter, thinner beater for softer notes and a heavier, thicker beater for a more piercing tone—although you can also play softly with a thicker beater, and generate a more full tone to boot. For a more muffled, even quieter tone, use a wooden beater.

You play the triangle by striking the beater against the outside edge near the middle of any of the three sides; I like to play the single fully enclosed side, but that's a personal preference. This produces the desired high-pitched ringing sound with lots of sustain. To cut the sustain, muffle the triangle by grabbing it near the strip with the thumb and first finger of the opposite (non-beater) hand. Many triangle parts require a mix of ringing and non-ringing notes; the open notes are notated with an ○ above the note, the muffled notes with a plus sign (+). It's also common to encounter staccato notation (little dots above the notes), which also indicates short, non-ringing tones.

The triangle part from Johannes Brahms's Symphony No. 4.

Playing a Roll

Another important technique is the triangle roll. This is a one-handed roll, achieved by repeatedly striking the beater on the *inside* of the triangle in the corner between two adjacent sides. Use an up-and-down or back-and-forth motion; use the very end of the beater for soft rolls, or play about a third of the way up the beater for louder ones.

A triangle roll is notated just like a snare drum or timpani roll, with three slashes through the note stem or above or below the note head. You may also find rolls notated with the trill mark.

Pro Tip
For faster passages, or as an optional approach to playing rolls, clip the triangle to a stand and use two beaters instead of one.

A Little Shake, a Little Roll: The Tambourine

Even though the tambourine is a Middle Eastern instrument, it's widely used in both orchestral and popular music.

Understanding the Tambourine

The tambourine consists of a round frame made from either wood or plastic. Pairs of small metal jingles (also called *zils*) are embedded in the frame, and they make their characteristic "jingle" sound when the tambourine is shaken or struck.

In orchestral work, you can find tambourines either with or without plastic or calfskin heads. In most instances, the head is tacked onto the tambourine's rim, although some models come with tunable heads. Although headless tambourines are perhaps more common in popular music, you're more likely to find headed models in orchestral music.

Orchestral headed tambourines.

(Photo courtesy of Latin Percussion.)

Playing a Headless Tambourine

There are two ways to play a headless tambourine. The first method involves shaking the tambourine back and forth in your hand. Most tambourines have an indented grip area, sometimes with a drilled finger hole. Grip the tambourine firmly in this area with one hand—but not too tight, as you want the jingles to vibrate freely. You can shake the tambourine with your hand only, using your wrist as a lever, or with your entire arm from the elbow down.

To create a more distinct "hit," strike the tambourine against the palm of your opposite hand, the gathered fingers of this hand, or your leg or hip. You can combine the shaking and hitting techniques by shaking the tambourine for unaccented notes and then striking it against your palm for accented notes.

The second way to play a headless tambourine is to strike it with a mallet or drumstick. For this technique, the tambourine is typically mounted on a stand, which enables you to play the tambourine with two sticks for faster passages.

Playing a Headed Tambourine

You play a headed tambourine in much the same fashion as a headless one. You can shake it or strike it, as the music requires. The big difference between headless and headed models comes in how you strike the tambourine. While you have to strike a headless tambourine on the rim, you have the option of striking a headed model either on the rim or on the head. This is where things get interesting.

Start by holding the tambourine more or less horizontal to the ground, so that it's positioned like a snare drum. While this isn't routine for playing popular music, it's the norm for orchestral work, and provides a good mix of playing flexibility and resonance.

When you strike the tambourine on its head, you can obtain a variety of different sounds depending on where on the head you strike it and with what you strike it. Strike near the middle of the head for a louder but less ringing sound; strike nearer the rim to pick up a little bit of ring.

You can strike the head with the palm of your hand for a full and loud sound, with the fingers of your hand for a very delicate sound, or with drumsticks or mallets for a more defined attack. Again, let the music determine how you approach the instrument for any give piece.

The tambourine part from Antonin Dvorak's Carnival Overture—*fast notes and loud shake rolls.*

Playing a Tambourine Roll

Then there's the tambourine roll, notated by the expected three slashes through the note or the trill mark. There are two ways to approach this. The simplest and easiest type of tambourine roll is achieved by holding the tambourine in one hand and rapidly rolling your hand back and forth, pivoting at the wrist. This creates a constant "jingle" from the instrument and is sufficient for much popular music.

Grace Note

You can play the one-handed tambourine roll on either a headed or headless tambourine.

In orchestral work, however, a much different type of tambourine roll is required. This type of roll, called a *thumb roll*, can be played only on headed tambourines—and is much more difficult to execute.

To play a thumb roll, start by holding the tambourine in your left hand. Next, wet your right thumb with your tongue or with wax, the better to ease the friction of the roll. You then position your thumb on the head of the tambourine, about a half-inch in from the rim at the six o'clock position. Press in against the head and then run your thumb around the edge of the tambourine, in the same direction your thumb is pointing (counterclockwise), at moderate speed. This will vibrate the tambourine's jingles, producing the roll.

Pro Tip

To produce a smoother thumb roll, put bee's wax on the head of the tambourine.

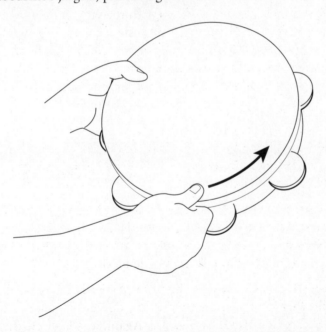

Playing a thumb roll on a headed tambourine.

Knock on Wood: Woodblocks and Temple Blocks

Now we come to a couple of wooden percussion instruments, both of which date back to the earliest log drums from prehistory. Of course, modern woodblocks and temple blocks are a far cry from those ancient drums carved from tree trunks—in fact, they may not even be made from wood anymore!

Playing the Woodblock

The woodblock is essentially a small but thick, rectangular piece of solid wood. There's typically a slit or larger cavity on one or both sides of the woodblock, which helps to tune the instrument and provide additional sustain.

While woodblocks have traditionally been made from wood (typically teak or some other hard wood), some companies are now making "woodblocks" made from plastic or composite material. The thought of using a non-wood woodblock may be anathema for many traditional percussionists, but if the ultimate goal is the sound, it may not matter which materials are used to construct the instrument.

Three different sizes of woodblocks.

(Photo courtesy of Latin Percussion.)

Pro Tip

Some woodblocks are designed to be mounted on a stand, typically with holes drilled for the mounting device that then clips onto a music stand or other percussion stand. You can also lay the woodblock on a table top or horizontal music stand and play the instrument with two mallets. To reduce unwanted vibrations, place a thin towel or other soft item between the woodblock and the stand.

Heads Up

Be careful when using plastic mallets. If you strike a woodblock too hard with a plastic mallet, you could crack the instrument.

To play the woodblock, lightly hold the bottom of the block in the palm of your left hand; you don't want your hand to dampen the instrument's sustain too much. Hold the mallet in your opposite hand and strike the woodblock pretty much dead center on top.

You play the woodblock by striking it with a hard rubber or plastic mallet or with a wooden stick. (In a pinch, you can strike it with a drumstick—the thinner the better.) Use a quick down-and-up motion; don't bury the mallet in the wood.

Playing Temple Blocks

The temple block is an Asian percussion instrument similar to the woodblock. Temple blocks are typically found in sets of five of different sizes. Each block is hollow with a slit through the middle or an opening on the playing side. The block's size gives it its own (indefinite) pitch—the larger the block, the lower the tone.

A modern set of plastic temple blocks.

(Photo courtesy of Latin Percussion.)

A set of temple blocks can be mounted all in a row (lowest on the right) or in a three-down, two-up configuration. Because of the pitch differences, temple blocks can be used to play rudimentary melodies. The sound of a temple block is more mellow and resonant than that of the harsher-sounding woodblock.

You typically play temple blocks with two rubber or hard yarn mallets. You strike each block on the top-center, using the expected quick down-and-up motion to maximize the tone and sustain.

Grace Note

Most modern temple blocks are made not from wood but from hard plastic.

Whip It Good: The Slapstick

A percussion slapstick is actually a kind of wooden whip, and it's used to create a loud whipping or snapping sound. The instrument is comprised of one long plank of wood with a second, shorter plank connected with a spring hinge. The longer plank functions as the handle.

A wooden slapstick.

(Photo courtesy of Toca/Latin Percussion.)

You typically play the slapstick one-handed. Hold the instrument in your primary hand with the shorter piece of wood pulled back, then snap this piece forward using your thumb. Alternately, you can hold the slapstick in one hand and force the short piece of wood down with your opposite hand.

Scraping It Together: Sandpaper Blocks

Here's an unusual little instrument—two sets of woodblocks with sandpaper attached. These are called, imaginatively enough, sandpaper blocks or sandblocks.

A set of sandpaper blocks.

Unlike other wooden blocks, you don't strike sandpaper blocks together or hit them with a mallet; instead, you rub them together in a back-and-forth motion. The rough sandpaper rubbing back and forth makes a scratching kind of sound, typically used to effect rhythmic patterns similar to "soft shoe" dancing.

Playing sandpaper blocks is quite easy. Hold one block in each hand, then use a back-and-forth motion to scrape the bottom sides of the two blocks together. Scrape slower for drawn–out, longer notes; scrape quickly for short, rapid notes.

Special Effects: The Ratchet

Here's another instrument that creates a scratchy, somewhat grating sound. The ratchet consists of a gear attached to a handle. When you turn the handle, the gear clicks against four thin pieces of wood inside the instrument. The result is a continuous clicking or rattling sound, typically used for special effects.

Turn the handle quickly for short, rapid notes. Turn the handle slowly to draw out the sound for longer notes.

The ratchet.

(Photo courtesy of Toca/ Latin Percussion.)

A Sustained Rattle: The Vibraslap

The vibraslap is an interesting instrument, somewhere in between a slapstick and ratchet. The sound produced is like a sustained rattle, but it's created by slapping the two parts of the instrument together.

The vibraslap has two parts, a wooden ball and a wooden box, the latter containing several loose-fitting metal pins. The two parts are connected via a bent metal rod.

To play the vibraslap, hold the end of the metal rod firmly in your left hand. Now use your right hand to slap the ball towards the box. This creates the sustained rattle that the instrument is known for.

Grace Note

The vibraslap is a modern variation of the *quijada*, a traditional Mexican instrument made from the jawbone of an ass.

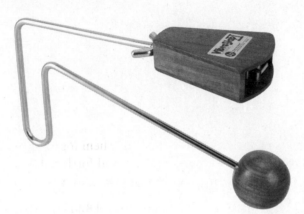

The vibraslap.

(Photo courtesy of Latin Percussion.)

Boing Boing: The Flexatone

The flexatone is another odd little percussion instrument, used primarily for special effects. It consists of a small sheet of flexible metal attached at one end to a handle; two wooden balls are mounted on either side of the sheet.

Hold the flexatone in one hand, with your palm around the handle and your thumb on the free end of the metal sheet. Shake the flexatone to hit the wooden balls against the sheet of metal, then use your thumb to bend the metal and bend the pitch, for a "boing" type of effect.

The flexatone.

(Photo courtesy of Latin Percussion.)

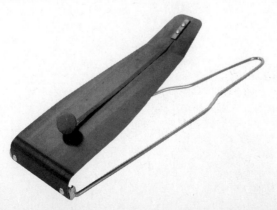

Shake It Up: Shakers

Want even more sustained noise? Then turn to a shaker—of which there are many in the percussion family. Generically, a shaker is a hollow metal, plastic, or wood tube with small beads or pellets inside that create a rattling sound when shaken. Most orchestral shakers are long cylinders.

You play a shaker by—surprise!—shaking it. You can hold a cylindrical shaker in one or both hands; shake it forward and back in a sharp motion to produce a distinct sound. Shake harder and sharper to produce accented notes.

A cylindrical shaker for both popular and orchestral work.

(Photo courtesy of Latin Percussion.)

Happy Holidays: Sleigh Bells

Here's another instrument that produces a highly distinctive sound. Sleigh bells—sometimes called *jingle bells*—are used to create the kind of sleigh bell sound heard in Christmas music around the world. The sound is also popular in orchestral works, typically for rhythmic effect.

Sleigh bells consist of multiple small bells, each with a small clapper inside. Some sleigh bells are attached to a short wrist strap; more commonly, the bells are attached to a wooden handle.

Sleigh bells.

(Photo courtesy of Latin Percussion.)

You play the sleigh bells by shaking them. There are two ways to do this. Most players simply pick the sleigh bells up by the handle and shake away, using the wrist and lower arm. If you want more control and precision, however, you should hold the sleigh bells upside down, with the handle on top. Grasp the handle in one hand and then hit the top of the handle with the other hand.

Pretty Sounds: Wind Chimes

You may have wind chimes hanging around your house, for decorative effect and background noise, but they're also a valid percussion instrument. Wind chimes are constructed from a series of small metal or wooden tubes; they sound when the tubes are excited and strike against each other.

You can play wind chimes with your hands or with a small metal or wooden beater. Move your hand or beater down the row of rods to produce the musical effect—typically a kind of *glissando* up or down the (indefinitely pitched) scale.

def•i•ni•tion

A **glissando** is a rapid series of consecutive tones moving up or down a scale.

Grace Note

Wind chimes used in orchestral work are more precisely called *chime trees* or *mark trees*. While civilian wind chimes can have any number of tubes arranged in different patterns (including circularly), chime trees are always ordered linearly.

A set of metal wind chimes.

(Photo courtesy of Latin Percussion.)

Not a Plant: The Bell Tree

A bell tree looks like its name: a small tree made up of nested metal bells or bowls. Each bell is tuned to a definite pitch; the sound of an individual bell is high and delicate.

You play the bell tree with a metal triangle beater or metal glockenspiel mallet. You can strike individual bells in the tree or, more commonly, slide the beater down the tree for a glissando effect.

Playing a bell tree.

(Photo courtesy of Latin Percussion.)

The Sound of Thor: The Thundersheet

A bell tree produces a delicate, pitched sound. Other metal percussion instruments produce less delicate, unpitched sounds—more like raw noise.

When you want the effect of thunder, strike a large metal plate called a *thundersheet*. A thundersheet is a thin sheet of metal, anywhere from two to three feet wide and high. The plate hangs vertically from a strap attached to a larger stand.

Thundersheets of different sizes.

(Photo courtesy of Sabian Cymbals.)

There are many ways to play a thundersheet. One approach is to hold and shake the bottom edge. Another approach is to strike the plate with a gong mallet or wooden chime mallet; use two mallets and roll slowly to achieve a rumbling effect. Still other scenarios require you to use a pair of drumsticks, which produces sounds from a low-pitched "ping" to the more characteristic thundering roar.

Pro Tip

More metallic sounds come from striking objects such as metal pipes, anvils, brake drums, and garbage can lids. Some of these are legitimate instruments sold by musical instrument companies; others are true "found objects" that are called into service as needed. Strike them with whatever makes the best tone.

Ethnic Percussion Instruments for Orchestral Use

The instruments discussed in this chapter aren't the only auxiliary percussion instruments used in concert and orchestral settings. Many orchestral works utilize a variety of ethnic percussion instruments, which are best discussed in those chapters specific to their regional origin. The most common of these orchestral ethnic instruments include the following:

- Bongos, discussed in Chapter 12
- Castanets, discussed in Chapter 12
- Congas, discussed in Chapter 12
- Cowbells, discussed in Chapter 12
- Finger cymbals, discussed in Chapter 14
- Maracas, discussed in Chapter 12
- Timbales, discussed in Chapter 12

Read ahead to learn more about these instruments.

Putting It All Together: The Percussion Ensemble

The percussion instruments discussed in this section are not only employed in orchestral use, but can also be part of the percussion ensemble. A percussion ensemble is just as the name implies: an ensemble consisting of various percussion instruments.

The word *various* is important when describing the percussion ensemble. There's no set grouping of instruments; any percussion instrument can be included, from timpani to snare drum to xylophone to bell tree. There's also no set size to the percussion ensemble, so pieces written for 3 players are just as common as those written for 10.

Another interesting aspect of the percussion ensemble is that it's quite common for any one player to play multiple instruments—in the same piece. Just as long as the composer gives the player time to switch from one instrument to another, this is a great way to add as many colors as possible using a minimal number of hands.

With all this in mind, I've included in this book a work for five-person percussion ensemble, titled *Into the West: A Short Piece for Percussion Ensemble.* The music for the piece is in Appendix B; the performance is the final track on the accompanying audio CD. This piece is scored for a variety of instruments, including timpani, xylophone, bass drum, snare drum, suspended cymbal, hand cymbals, triangle, tambourine, and assorted auxiliary instruments. It's easy enough to be played by junior high and high school percussionists, and serves to demonstrate how the various percussion instruments sound and work together.

The Least You Need to Know

♦ The modern orchestra includes parts of all manner of small, auxiliary percussion instruments.

♦ The triangle is struck with a thin metal beater.

♦ The tambourine can be shaken or struck—or, in the case of headed models, rolled with your thumb.

♦ Woodblocks and temple blocks are similar in construction and in how they're played.

♦ Other popular auxiliary percussion instruments include the slapstick, sandpaper blocks, ratchet, shakers, sleigh bells, wind chimes, bell tree, and thundersheet.

♦ All these instruments—as well as the main orchestral percussion instruments—can be employed in percussion ensembles.

Part 3

The World of Marching Percussion

Marching bands and drum corps introduce some new approaches to traditional percussion instruments. In these chapters, you learn all about marching drums and cymbals, as well as bells and other mallet instruments used on the march—or in the pit.

Chapter 8

Marching Drums and Cymbals

In This Chapter

- Getting familiar with marching percussion—and drum corps playing
- Powering up the marching snare drum
- Learning to play the tenor drums
- Pounding away at the marching bass drum
- Crashing and splashing the marching cymbals

In this section of the book, we examine those percussion instruments used in drum corps and marching bands. To some degree, these are the same instruments used in concert and orchestral settings; after all, a bass drum is a bass drum is a bass drum, right?

Well, not exactly. Yes, all bass drums feature the same construction and serve similar roles, but the kind of bass drum you find in a marching environment is subtly different from that found in a concert environment—and from the bass drum that anchors your everyday drum set. Not only is the bass drum itself a little different, the technique you use to play it is also different.

With that in mind, then, let's look at the drums and cymbals used in marching bands and drum corps—what they are and how they're played.

Understanding Marching Percussion

There are four main components of most marching bands and drum corps, and an optional fifth component. The sections you're likely to find in any band include:

- Snare drums, often in multiple parts (Snare I, Snare II, and so on)
- Tenor drums, which are like concert toms, typically carried in groups of three or more

◆ Bass drums, often with more than one part (Bass I, Bass II, and so on)

◆ Cymbals, of the hand-crashed variety

 These four sections are collectively known as the drumline or battery. I've included a short performance from a typical drumline on the CD, so you can hear how all these instruments sound when played together.

The fifth, optional component is that of melodic percussion—xylophone, marimba, glockenspiel, and so forth. While glockenspiels can be carried, the other mallet instruments are part of a non-marching "pit," located directly in front of the audience on the performing field.

Grace Note _____

The pit isn't limited to melodic percussion instruments. It can also include drum sets, electric guitars, bass guitars, and the like. Learn more about pit percussion in Chapter 9.

Marching instruments differ from concert instruments in that they're portable, of course, typically carried on some sort of shoulder-mounted harness. In addition, today's marching percussion instruments are built for power—they're loud, cutting, and durable enough to stand up to extreme use and abuse. In fact, if you're familiar with marching bands from years gone by, you'll find today's instruments even louder and heavier-duty than what were common 20 or more years ago.

You'll also find that music for marching bands and drum corps is more sophisticated than it used to be. In addition to the expected marches and cadences, you'll find adaptations of orchestral pieces, movie soundtracks, Broadway musical scores, and the like. This requires more sophisticated technique and greater skill from the entire percussion section; drum corps players, in particular, are every bit as talented as their orchestral cousins.

Grace Note _____

There are marching bands, with which most of us are familiar, and then there are drum corps, which are superficially similar but totally different beasts. The world of competitive drum corps is both fun and demanding. Most corps travel around a region (or across the country) performing their meticulously rehearsed shows on football fields before large crowds and panels of judges.

Because of the competition, drum corps are more musically (and theatrically) demanding than traditional marching bands. At the beginning of each season, a drum corps prepares a new show, typically between 10 and 12 minutes long. The musical content can vary wildly both between and within shows, running the gamut from symphonic works to Broadway tunes to rock and roll to Latin and other ethnic music.

Drum corps percussion parts are intricate and difficult and require a high level of skill to execute. This type of playing isn't for the amateur or the undedicated; you need great chops to get into the corps and much practice to perfect your part. The fact that you have to execute these demanding parts while marching in complex formations just adds to the challenge. For this reason, many drummers consider drum corps the high point of their careers; it's certainly one of the most demanding!

Getting to Know the Marching Snare Drum

We'll start our examination of the marching percussion section with the snare drum. As with most other types of music, marching music puts the snare section front and center, driving the entire section—and the entire band.

Most marching bands have multiple snare drummers, playing one or more different parts. Large high school and college bands are likely to have anywhere from a half-dozen to a dozen snares; a snare line of 7 to 10 players is common in a modern drum corps.

Deconstructing the Marching Snare

The marching snare drum is like an oversized concert snare. Head size is the same (14 inches in diameter is most common, although some drums have a smaller 13-inch head), but the depth of the drum extends to 10, 11, or even 12 inches. This extra depth enhances the drum's tone and volume level, making for some very loud drums.

A 14"×12" marching snare drum with free-floating heads.

(Photo courtesy of Ludwig/Musser Percussion.)

Most current-generation marching snares use a free-floating head assembly. Instead of the head being tensioned directly to the shell, it's tensioned to a metal ring that sits on top of the shell. Because the tension is applied to the ring rather than the shell, you can tension the head extremely tightly without breaking the more fragile wooden shell.

This high head tensioning is another unique feature of the marching snare drum. Today's marching percussion sections tension their instruments extremely high, much higher than with concert or drum set snares, resulting in a super-tight batter head. This allows for fast sticking (tight heads equal lots of rebound) and a piercing, almost popping sound.

To take the dual abuse of high tensioning and hard hits (with big sticks), marching drum heads are more durable than similar heads for concert snare drums. Marching heads are made from Mylar, Kevlar, and other plastic fibers; the result is a waterproof, bulletproof, nearly indestructible head that will hold up under virtually all conditions.

Choosing Marching Sticks

Here's another big difference between playing in an orchestra and playing in a marching band: Concert snare drummers use relatively thin sticks, and marching snare drummers use relatively thick ones.

In fact, marching snare sticks are the fattest and longest available today. The extra size is necessary to coax all available volume from the drum, and also to hold up under extreme playing conditions. (You don't want your sticks breaking in the middle of a half-time show or parade!) The 3S is the most common stick type, although there are lots of similarly thick sticks available.

As to the other features of the stick, that's still a personal preference. Marching sticks are available with round or traditional beads made from wood or nylon; the sticks themselves are made from the expected variety of woods.

Playing the Snare

Grace Note

Learn more about traditional and matched grip in Chapter 3.

Marching snare technique is identical to that for concert playing. Both traditional grip and matched grip are acceptable, with the provision that all the players in a drumline use the same grip. For this reason, it's important to find out what grip is used by your school's marching band or your desired drum corps. You don't want to be the only matched-grip player auditioning for a line that uses all traditional grip.

That said, traditional grip appears to be more popular these days than matched grip, especially with the major drum corps. But not all corps use traditional grip, so again it's wise to learn both grips and use the one you need to use with a particular ensemble.

One thing that is different about playing marching snare, however, is the volume level. You're not playing indoors in a concert hall with perfect acoustics; you're playing outside, where all the sound goes up, up, and away. You need to learn how to play loud while maintaining the necessary speed and technique. That's part of what marching playing is all about.

Another difference between orchestral and marching playing concerns the roll—in particular, the open roll. Open rolls are much more common in marching music than in orchestral music; in fact, unless the music is notated otherwise, you can pretty much assume that any roll you encounter is an open one.

A final difference in marching drumming is the sticking. Unlike in orchestral music, where the sticking you play is relatively unimportant (what matters is the sound you create), in marching bands and especially drum corps, it's important for all the drummers in a section to play with the same sticking. When everybody is playing their lefts and rights at precisely the same time, a unique visual effect is created. Of course, this type of precision also requires a lot of practice—so get your chops in shape!

> **Pro Tip**
>
> There is a unique visual component to drum corps and marching band playing today. In particular, snare drummers should learn *back sticking*, where you flip the butt of the stick through to strike the head of the drum. Also common are *stick clicks*, where you strike one stick on the other high above the drum.

Learning the Rudiments

Precise technique is necessary when playing both concert and marching snare. But marching music makes more prominent use of the drum rudiments than does most orchestral music, so marching drummers need to have a command of these essential snare drum patterns.

> **Grace Note** _____
>
> The traditional drum rudiments date all the way back to the 1600s, from Switzerland's fife and drum corps of that day. These basic rudiments evolved over time (and through several countries), until 26 of them were certified as the official rudiments of the National Association of Rudimental Drummers (NARD). When NARD eventually disbanded, the Percussive Arts Society expanded the list to the 40 rudiments we recognize today.

There are 40 snare drum rudiments recognized by the Percussive Arts Society (PAS). These rudiments, dubbed the PAS/40, are the building blocks of all marching snare drum parts; all drummers—marching drummers especially—need to master all 40 of these patterns.

The following table details the 40 PAS rudiments. Practice them from slow to fast and back again, gradually speeding up the tempo as you master each pattern.

> **Grace Note** _____
>
> Learn more about playing these rudiments in my companion book, *The Complete Idiot's Guide to Playing Drums, Second Edition* (Alpha Books, 2004).

The 40 Snare Drum Rudiments

Rudiment	As Written
1. Single-stroke roll	♩ ♩ ♩ ♩ ♩ ♩ ♩ ♩ ♫♫♫♫♫♫ R L R L R L R L R L R L R L R L RLRL RLRL RLRLRLRL
2. Single-stroke four	♫♫♫ ♫♫♫ R L R L R L R L
3. Single-stroke seven	♫♫♫♫♩ R L R L R L R

continues

The 40 Snare Drum Rudiments (continued)

Rudiment	As Written
4. Multiple-bounce roll	
5. Triple-stroke roll	
6. Double-stroke open roll	
7. Five-stroke roll	
8. Six-stroke roll	
9. Seven-stroke roll	
10. Nine-stroke roll	
11. Ten-stroke roll	
12. Eleven-stroke roll	
13. Thirteen-stroke roll	
14. Fifteen-stroke roll	
15. Seventeen-stroke roll	
16. Single paradiddle	
17. Double paradiddle	
18. Triple paradiddle	
19. Single paradiddle-diddle	
20. Flam	
21. Flam accent	
22. Flam tap	

Rudiment	As Written
23. Flamacue	L R L R L LR R L R L R R L
24. Flam paradiddle	L R L R R R L R L L
25. Single-flammed mill	LR R L R rL L R L
26. Flam paradiddle-diddle	L R L R R L L RL R L L R R
27. Pataflafla	LR L RrL LR L RrL
28. Swiss Army triplet	L R R L L R R L / R L L R rL L R
29. Inverted flam tap	L R L R L R
30. Flam drag	L R LL R rL R R L
31. Drag	LL R R R L
32. Single-drag tap	LL R L R R L R
33. Double-drag tap	LL R LL R L R rL R rL R / LL R LL R L R rL R rL R
34. Lesson 25	LL R L R LL R L R
35. Single dragadiddle	R R L R R L LL R L L
36. Drag paradiddle #1	R LL R L R R L rL R L L
37. Drag paradiddle #2	R LL R LL R L R R L rL R rL R L L
38. Single ratamacue	LL R L R L rR L R L R
39. Double ratamacue	LL R LL R L R L rR L R rL R L R
40. Triple ratamacue	LL R LL R LL R L R L rR L rR L rL R L R

The first three rudiments are rolls played with single strokes, not the customary doubles. The fourth rudiment, the multiple-bounce roll, is the standard closed or buzz roll; the PAS notates it with a little "Z" over the note rather than the traditional three slashes, but it's the same thing.

Rudiments 6 through 15 are traditional open rolls of various lengths. Note that the six-stroke roll is an odd beast with a second tap at the end of the roll; it's like a five-stroke roll with an extra ending note.

The "diddle" rudiments (16 through 19, plus 24, 26, 35, 36, and 37) are all about the sticking. A simple paradiddle is two singles and a double, either RLRR or LRLL. All the other "diddles" are variations of this.

> **Grace Note** _____
>
> My favorite oddball rudiment is rudiment number 34, dubbed "Lesson 25." This dates back to the pre-PAS rudiments, which were 26 similar patterns authorized by the National Association of Rudimental Drummers (NARD). The 25th NARD rudiment was the aforementioned Lesson 25; when the NARD rudiments were supplanted by the PAS rudiments, this rudiment kept its name but not its position. As I said, this rudiment is a little oddball.

Introducing the Tenor Drums

The next drum in the marching percussion line is the tenor drum—more accurately, the tenor _drums_, plural. In marching use, tenor drums are single-headed drums, with no snares or heads on the bottom, much like concert drums in orchestral use. Most tenor rigs include three to six drums, which are most commonly played with drumsticks—although hard mallets are used on occasion.

Most small marching bands have only one or two tenor players in the lineup. Larger marching bands and drum corps incorporate lines with up to a half-dozen tenors.

Deconstructing the Tenor Drums

> **Grace Note** _____
>
> Tenor drums are sometimes called _toms, trios, quads, quints,_ or _hexes_—depending on the number of drums attached to a single marching harness.

A tenor setup typically consists of three to six individual drums, sized from 8- to 14-inch in diameter. The four-drum setup is most common, with drums sized either 8, 10, 12, and 13 inches, or the larger 10-, 12-, 13-, and 14-inch arrangement. These multiple drums are mounted on a single harness, so the drummer can play between multiple drums.

Tenor drums can be made of wood, carbon fiber, or other common shell materials. The bottom of most tenor drums is cut at a slight angle, to enable the sound to project in front of the player toward the audience.

A set of four marching tenor drums (quads).

(Photo courtesy of Pearl Drums.)

Interestingly, tenor drums are not arranged in ascending or descending order on the harness. In a four-drum (quad) configuration, the lowest drum is on the far left, the next lowest on the far right, the second highest on the near left, and the highest on the near right. For five-drum setups, the fifth (and highest) drum is placed between the two high drums in the middle of the rig; the sixth drum in a six-drum setup is placed similarly.

A typical quad configuration—not the traditional "large to small" order.

Tenor drums, like concert drums, are indefinite pitched drums. Their tuning, however, can approximate specific intervals between the drums. Thirds and fourths are the most common intervals between drums.

In terms of tuning, tenor drums are typically tensioned extremely tight—much like the marching snare drum. Tenor drums don't produce a low "thud," but rather a high, pinging "thwack," especially on the smaller drums. The high tuning also results in a very responsive head surface, ideal for fast sticking and other sophisticated playing techniques.

Playing Tenor Drums

You play the tenor drum with either large drumsticks or mallets. The mallets can be of any type, with wood, plastic, rubber, and felt heads all common.

That said, most tenor players today use sticks instead of mallets. That's because modern tenor drum parts resemble snare drum parts, but on multiple drums. The typical tenor drum part includes rolls and rudiments and rim shots and the like, as well as some very fast stickings. Combine these techniques with the high-pitched sound of tightly tensioned tenor drums, and you have a very versatile instrument.

Whether playing with sticks or mallets, all tenor drummers use matched grip, which affords the best reach to all the drums in the setup. The down-and-up stroke is identical to that used with the snare drum or concert toms. Strike each drum not in the center, but rather midway between the center and rim, as with timpani. You'll also need to learn some crossover sticking, to play patterns between the differently pitched drums.

Grace Note

Because of the arrangement of the drums in a tenor drum setup, creative sticking often comes into play—that is, how best to navigate through a part given the layout of the drums.

In many bands and corps, it's the melodic nature of the tenor drums that add the distinctive flavor to cadences and grooves. The tenors are used for more than just timekeeping; there's a lot of musicality involved. It's also a difficult instrument to play, requiring the same sort of sophisticated rudimental technique as the snare drum but with added multi-drum technique. You have to read and play not only rhythms, but also different pitches on the staff.

A typical tenor drum part—different pitches for different drums.

Working with Marching Bass Drums

 Marching bass drums are much smaller than concert bass drums. In fact, today's marching basses are smaller than those older drummers might remember from their youth. And there are more of them.

In the old days (20 or so years ago), a marching band might have just one or two bass drummers, both playing the same-sized drum (large). Not so today; the typical marching band or drum corps might have as many as four to six bass drummers, playing drums of various sizes.

Deconstructing the Marching Bass Drum

The typical marching band or drum corps bass line consists of multiple bass drums, each of a different size. This enables the section to play complex tonal passages—some might even say a "melody," if only the drums were of definite pitch (which they're not).

Marching bass drums of various sizes.

(Photo courtesy of Pearl Drums.)

As such, marching bass drums come in a variety of sizes—all somewhat smaller than the marching basses of yesteryear. Head sizes range from 14 to 32 inches, with shell depth of 14 inches (or 16 inches for the larger-headed drums). The larger drums play the lower notes, of course.

Marching bass drums are typically of wood ply construction. The drum is mounted on a shoulder harness and played vertically, with the two heads to the left and right of the drummer.

Playing the Marching Bass Drum

Each drummer in the bass line typically plays a separate part. So if there are five bass drummers, there are five bass drum parts, one drummer to a part.

Bass drummers play with two hard felt mallets. Both heads are played (the right head with the right hand, the left head with the left hand), which makes the marching bass drum unique in having two batter heads.

A typical bass drum mallet with a hard felt head.

(Photo courtesy of Pro-Mark.)

The proper stroke is with a combination of forearm and wrist, placing the mallet dead center in the head. Playing rapid strokes between hands for complex rhythmic patterns is common.

Crashing the Marching Cymbals

Cymbals in a marching band are hand cymbals, not suspended ones. The cymbal player holds one cymbal in each hand and crashes them together.

Deconstructing the Marching Cymbal

Marching cymbals are quite similar to orchestral hand cymbals. Each set consists of a matched pair of cymbals of equal weight and size. Cymbals range in size from 12 to 20 inches, with 16 and 18 inches being most common; larger sizes are more difficult to handle when marching. Weight is either medium or medium heavy.

Most drum corps and larger marching bands have large cymbal lines, with different players playing cymbals of different sizes. All sorts of flashy visual effects are possible, including cymbal twirls, but more important are the variations in sound possible with this type of line. Some pieces include long cymbal "breaks," where the cymbal line goes solo to show its stuff. It's actually kind of impressive, both visually and musically.

A set of 16-inch marching cymbals from Paiste.

(Photo courtesy of Paiste Cymbals.)

Playing Marching Cymbals

Grace Note

Learn more about playing the full crash in Chapter 5, "Cymbals and Gongs."

As with orchestral hand cymbals, each marching cymbal is attached to a leather grip and pad. You hold one cymbal in each hand, vertically, and crash them together in various ways.

We'll start with the full crash. This is played just as you do in a concert setting, by bringing the two cymbals together and then apart in a glancing stroke. The farther apart you start, the louder the crash.

Unlike in concert playing, where you don't rotate the cymbals forward when done, many marching bands and drum corps feature elaborate cymbal "choreography," full of all sorts of flashy hand movements. Some of these movements rotate the cymbals forward and backward and every which way, which looks cool even if it doesn't do much for the sound.

The short marching crash.

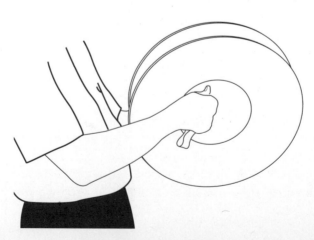

Also common in marching music is the soft crash or marching crash. This is more of a "splash" sound used to accompany the bass drum on a repeated quarter-note beat. For this sound, keep the two cymbals close together, with one cymbal held about an inch higher than the other one. Strike the topmost cymbal inward and down into the bottom cymbal in a short, sliding motion, letting the full edge surfaces hit together. Repeat this stroke in the opposite direction for the next note, and so on.

The Least You Need to Know

- ◆ Marching percussion is similar to orchestral percussion, but more portable and capable of producing louder sounds.

- ◆ The marching snare drum is deeper than the concert snare with much higher (tighter) tuning.

- ◆ Tenor drums are like concert toms on a marching harness, used to play multiple tones.

- ◆ Most marching bands and drum corps use four or more bass drums of varying sizes.

- ◆ Hand-held marching cymbals are used both for full and soft crashes.

Marching Bells and Mallets

In This Chapter

- ◆ Getting to know the instruments of the front ensemble

- ◆ Learning to play the marching glockenspiel

- ◆ Understanding the differences between marching and concert mallet instruments

Modern drum corps and some marching bands utilize more than just drums and cymbals. Mallet percussion, in the form of a front ensemble or pit (as distinct from the drumline or battery), is now a common feature of most corps and larger bands, adding a little melody to the traditional drum rhythms.

Introducing the Front Ensemble

The name *front ensemble* comes from where these larger, non-portable percussion instruments are placed: on the front sideline of the football field, directly in front of the stands at the 50-yard line. The pit, as it's also called, contains not just percussion instruments, but any instrument that can't be carried or marched with. In terms of non-percussion instruments, that typically means amplified instruments, such as keyboards, synthesizers, and electric guitar and bass.

Percussion instruments in the pit typically include some or all of the standard mallet percussion, including xylophone, vibraphone, marimba, and glockenspiel. Some front ensembles add timpani, concert bass drums, congas, timbales, chimes, gongs, and suspended cymbals. It's also not uncommon to add a full drum set to the pit.

The front ensemble is a relatively recent development in the marching field, arriving in drum corps competition in 1982. Prior to this time, some corps positioned a single timpanist on the 50-yard line or incorporated bulky marching timpani and keyboard instruments. Wiser heads prevailed, however, and now color is added by rolling concert instruments to the sideline prior to performance.

Horizontal Bells: The Marching Glockenspiel

We'll start our examination of marching mallet percussion with one that predates the development of the front ensemble. The marching glockenspiel or bell lyre is a close cousin to the orchestral glockenspiel. The main difference is that the marching version is tilted 90 degrees, held vertically, and played with a single mallet in one hand. (The other hand is used to support the instrument in its carrier.) The lowest notes are at the bottom and the highest at the top.

A trio of marching glockenspiels.

(Photo courtesy of Ludwig/Musser Percussion.)

The glockenspiel is unique among the melodic percussion instruments in that it can be and often is used outside of the front ensemble. In marching bands, especially, it's common to find several glockenspiel players marching in line with the rest of the band, which is easy enough as the instrument is more portable than a marimba or xylophone.

You play the marching glockenspiel with a brass or plastic mallet; brass produces a more piercing, bell-like sound. You use the same technique as with the concert version—minus the left hand, of course. That means no rolls or fast passages, save for what you can execute with a single mallet.

Grace Note

Learn more about the glockenspiel and other concert melodic percussion instruments in Chapter 6.

Horizontal Mallets: Xylophones, Marimbas, and Vibraphones

The other melodic percussion instruments in the front ensemble are the same horizontal keyboard instruments you find in a concert band or orchestra: xylophone, marimba, and (sometimes) vibraphone. The marching versions of these instruments are pretty much identical to their concert cousins, with a handful of minor exceptions.

The first difference comes in the instruments' stand. While most concert mallet instruments come on rolling stands, the castors are relatively small and discreet. Not so with the marching versions, which come on carts with oversized, heavy-duty wheels. This makes it easier to roll the instruments onto and off of the field.

> **Grace Note**
>
> While our focus is on front ensemble instruments, true "marching" xylophones and marimbas do exist. These are smaller instruments, typically with two to two-and-a-half octaves and smaller bars, that are carried horizontally in front of the player on a shoulder harness. As you might expect, even at a reduced size, these are still large and unwieldy instruments, difficult to carry and march with—which is why they're seeing diminishing use today.

Three-octave and four-octave marimbas designed for front ensemble use; note the oversized wheels.

(Photo courtesy of Ludwig/ Musser Percussion.)

The second difference comes in the instruments' composition. Where most concert xylophones and marimbas have bars made from rosewood, most marching instruments have bars made from synthetic materials, such as Kelon. These synthetic materials hold up better in the elements and won't be damaged if it starts to rain or snow during a performance.

The third difference is that you're more likely to see smaller instruments than larger ones in the front ensemble. Whereas four-octave (and larger) marimbas are common in concert use, for example, many drum corps use three-octave (or smaller) marimbas in their pits. It's a matter of convenience; it's easier to roll a smaller instrument around than a larger one.

The final difference between concert and marching instruments is that some marching keyboard instruments are "tricked out" to hold other auxiliary percussion instruments. That is, the frame is adapted with racks and holders for cymbals, cowbells, woodblocks, you name it—anything small that may need to be played over the course of a routine. So a marching marimba may come to resemble the rolling cart of a one-man band, with the marimba player called upon to do double, triple, or quadruple duty with all these various instruments.

A Musser marimba with racks for auxiliary percussion instruments.

(Photo courtesy of Ludwig/Musser Percussion.)

The Least You Need to Know

◆ Many drum corps and marching bands place non-portable percussion instruments in a stationary front ensemble or pit.

◆ Front-ensemble instruments can include glockenspiel, xylophone, marimba, and vibraphone—as well as concert bass drum, timpani, and gongs.

◆ The marching glockenspiel is a vertically held version of the horizontal concert glockenspiel, played with just one mallet.

◆ Marching xylophones and marimbas are typically made with synthetic bars, have heavy-duty wheels, and can come with racks to hold additional small percussion instruments.

Part 4

The World of Popular Percussion

Just what is popular percussion? It all starts with the drum set, in all its many variations. But it also includes the instruments of the drum circle—which anybody can play.

Drum Set

In This Chapter

- ◆ The pieces and parts of the modern drum set
- ◆ How to play the drum set
- ◆ Basic beats and fills
- ◆ Moving beyond sticks
- ◆ Reading notated drum music

With orchestral and marching percussion out of the way, let's move on to percussion instruments used in today's popular music, starting with the drum set. The drum set is a combination of different types of drums and cymbals, played by a single drummer. Even though it's assembled from other percussion instruments, the drum set is an instrument in and of itself—and a handful to play!

Getting to Know the Drum Set

A drum set is, literally, a set of drums—and cymbals and stands and assorted other odds and ends. There is no "standard" drum set; a drummer can assemble a set from any number of pieces and arrange them any way he or she sees fit.

A drum set is typically described as having a certain number of "pieces," where each piece is a separate drum. (You don't count cymbals or stands as pieces.) For example, a set with a snare drum, a bass drum, one small tom, and one large tom is a four-piece set; add a second tom (small or large), and you have a five-piece set.

Grace Note

When describing a drum set, "up" refers to small toms (mounted "up" over the bass drum) and "down" refers to large toms (placed "down" on the floor). So a two-up, one-down set has two small toms and one large tom.

There are no right or wrong setups, but certain setups are more common than others:

♦ Four-piece, with snare drum, bass drum, one small tom, and one large tom. Typically accompanied by a hi-hat and two or three cymbals. This is probably the most common setup today, among both rock and jazz drummers.

♦ Five-piece (two-up, one-down), with snare drum, bass drum, two small toms, and one large tom. Typically accompanied by a hi-hat and two or three cymbals. This is a popular configuration for beginning-level kits and with rock drummers.

♦ Five-piece (one-up, two-down), with snare drum, bass drum, one small tom, and two large toms. Typically accompanied by a hi-hat and two or three cymbals. This setup was originally popularized by big band drummers such as Gene Krupa and Buddy Rich, but has been recently embraced by rock drummers channeling the spirit of the late John Bonham, the original drummer for Led Zeppelin.

♦ Six-piece, with snare drum, bass drum, two small toms, and two large toms. Typically accompanied by a hi-hat and three or more cymbals. This setup is popular among studio, jazz/rock, and smooth jazz drummers—as well as any drummer who wants a lot of tonal options.

The four-piece kit popularized by the Beatles' Ringo Starr— Ludwig's "Liverpool 4" set.

(Photo courtesy of Ludwig/Musser Percussion.)

Another popular configuration—Pearl's five-piece Masters Custom kit.

(Photo courtesy of Pearl Drums.)

A six-piece kit from Drum Workshop—lots of toms (including suspended large toms) and lots of cymbals.

(Photo courtesy of Drum Workshop.)

Drum Set Drums

There are three types of drums in a drum set—the snare drum, the tom-toms, and the bass drum.

The Snare Drum

The snare drum is the most familiar drum in the kit, and arguably the most important. Most snare drums are 14 inches in diameter; the typical depth for a snare used in a drum set is in the 4.5- to 5.5-inch range, although deeper drums (6 inches or more) are sometimes employed for a fatter, deeper sound.

Snare drums for drum set use can be made from any type of material. Wood (either solid-shell or multiple-ply) of various types is always popular, as are shells of steel, brass, bronze, and other metals. Some drummers say that wood snares have a warmer sound, although I've always found that aluminum-shelled drums, like Ludwig's popular Supra-Phonic model, can be tuned for both a big or small sound.

Pro Tip

Some drummers use smaller, 12- or 13-inch snare drums (either as a main drum or as a supplemental drum, set to the left of the main snare) to produce a higher-pitched sound with a lot of "crack."

The Tom-Toms

Drum set tom-toms are like orchestral concert toms and marching tenor drums. They're two-headed drums with deep shells and no snare assembly underneath.

Tom-toms provide a drum set's color. A typical set has two or more toms; the more you have, the more options you have when playing fills or solos around the set.

Toms mounted above your bass drum—even if they're hanging from or sitting on a separate stand—are called small toms or riding toms. Small toms are available in diameters between 8 and 14 inches; if you have multiple small toms, a 2- or 3-inch difference between the toms provides the best tonal balance. The drums can either be attached to a mount on the top of the bass drum, or on freestanding stands (like cymbal stands, but for toms); some drummers mount a single small tom on a snare drum stand.

Where small toms are mounted directly in front of you, large toms are mounted off to your side. They're also larger than small toms, typically with diameters of 14, 16, or even 18 inches. Large toms are usually fitted with three legs, which is why they're often called *floor toms*. A newer trend is to suspend large toms from a stand, just like small toms; this is especially popular with smaller, shallower toms.

The Bass Drum

The bass drum is the punch at the bottom of the drum kit, the "boom-boom-boom" that drives the music forward, works with the bass player to establish a groove, and kicks out important accents. It's the foundation of the set.

What size bass drum you choose depends on the type of playing you're doing. If you're playing in an acoustic jazz group, go with a smaller, punchier drum with a 18- or 20-inch diameter head. For rock and pop music, 22-inch heads are quite versatile, with drum depth anywhere from 14 to 18 inches. (The deeper the drum, the deeper the punch.) If you're playing heavy metal or other arena rock music, go all the way up to a 24-inch bass—which is also a popular size with older-style big band drummers, as it produces a very loud, "boomy" sound.

Pro Tip

Some drummers like larger sets with two bass drums, which enable all manner of fast footwork. The double-bass sound can also be created via use of a double-bass pedal on a single bass drum; the pedal uses two footboards (one positioned by your hi-hat) to drive two bass drum beaters on the single drum.

Drum Set Cymbals

A drum set is more than just drums, of course—it also contains several cymbals. Drum set cymbals are made from cast or stamped brass and are available in a mind-staggering number of different sizes and weights.

Every set should have at least one of these three basic types of cymbals:

- **Ride.** This is a larger, heavier cymbal—typically in the 20- to 22-inch diameter range—on which you play a straight-eighth backing pattern (for rock) or a jazz ride pattern. A good ride cymbal has a relatively clean *attack* with a defined stick "ping," without a lot of built-up overtones or "wash."

- **Crash.** These are smaller, thinner cymbals—typically in the 16- to 18-inch range—that you hit hard to accentuate important points in the music. A good crash cymbal has a defined attack without being too overpowering.

- **Hi-hat.** This is a pair of cymbals—typically 14 inches in diameter—that you click together with your left foot via a hi-hat pedal. You can strike the hi-hat either closed (clicked together) or open (left slightly open, for more of a "splashy" sound).

def•i•ni•tion

Attack is the initial sound made when you hit a drum or cymbal—as opposed to the ring or "after tone." A "clean" or "defined" attack produces a clearly distinguished sound and more resonance from the instrument, where a "muddy" or "mushy" attack tends to blend more into the general mix.

A basic setup might have four cymbals—a 20-inch ride cymbal, two crash cymbals (16 and 18 inches), and a hi-hat. (Technically, the hi-hat counts as two cymbals, but you get the drift.)

Pro Tip

There are also various special-effect cymbals, such as *splash* cymbals (small, thin, and splashy-sounding), *sizzle* cymbals (a ride cymbal with rivets, for a sustained "sizzling" sound), and *china* cymbals (thin cymbals with an inverted edge that you play upside down for a "trashy" ride or crash sound). These special-effect cymbals, while useful in special circumstances, are not necessary in a basic setup.

The cymbal type to some degree defines the cymbal size; ride cymbals are larger cymbals than crashes. Cymbal size also affects the pitch; the larger the cymbal, the deeper the pitch. Cymbal thickness is also important, with thinner cymbals having a faster attack and a quicker decay (and a brighter sound) and thicker cymbals having more overtones and a longer, louder ring (and a darker sound).

Drum Set Stands

To put all this equipment in its place, the drum set incorporates a variety of stands and pedals, including the following:

♦ A snare-drum stand, which holds the snare in a type of "bucket" between your legs.

♦ Cymbal stands, in either straight or "boom" designs. (Boom stands use an angled section to place a cymbal closer in than is possible with a straight stand.)

♦ A hi-hat stand, which holds the two hi-hat cymbals and has a pedal you control with your left foot.

♦ Tom-tom stands, which hold small or large toms.

♦ Multi-stands, which combine two or more standard stand functions. (For example, Drum Workshop makes multi-stands that hold two toms and a cymbal boom—very space-efficient!)

Two more pieces of equipment are essential to any drum kit. The *bass drum pedal* moves a beater that strikes the batter head of your bass drum and is typically played with your right foot (on a right-handed set). And the *drum throne* is what you sit on—so make sure you get a comfortable one!

Playing the Drum Set

Even if you're a competent orchestral or marching snare drummer, playing the drum set is something else entirely. That's because you're using your entire body; instead of playing with just your hands, you're using both your hands and your feet. And that requires a lot of coordination!

Setting Up the Kit

Drum set playing starts with proper positioning behind the kit. You should position the drum throne directly behind the bass drum, so that you can reach the bass drum pedal without stretching. The throne should be positioned high enough that your knees are bent no more than 90 degrees, but low enough that the throne carries most of your weight.

Sitting on the throne, place your right foot (if you're playing right-handed) on the bass drum pedal, then spread your legs at about a 45-degree angle. Legs in position, place your hi-hat pedal under your left foot and your snare drum stand directly between your legs.

A typical five-piece setup—for right-handed players.

With your snare drum in place, adjust the height of the stand to a comfortable level, a few inches above the top of your legs. Most drummers leave the snare drum flat, although some like to tilt it toward them (to avoid accidental *rimshots*) or away from them (to facilitate deliberate rimshots). If you play traditional grip, you may want to tilt the snare from left to right to make it easier to play rimshots with your left hand.

If you're playing a single small tom, position it above the bass drum in front of and just above the snare drum. If you have a second small tom, position it to the right of the first tom. The large tom should be positioned to your right, opposite the snare drum and on the same plane.

As to the cymbals, the only rule is that you should position them within easy reach. In particular, your ride cymbal should be *very* easy to reach with your right hand, since you'll be playing it a lot. If you only have one small tom, the ride cymbal can be placed to its left above the bass drum. If you have two small toms, the ride cymbal will probably have to be positioned higher and farther to the right.

Crash cymbals are typically placed adjacent to and above the ride cymbal and to the left of the first small tom. You may or may not want to angle your crashes (that's a matter of personal preference), but you'll find that you get a more forceful crash if you have to reach for them a little.

Drum Set Sticks

Choosing the right drumstick is a very personal decision, especially for the drum set. If you play a lot of soft music or jazz, you may want a thinner, lighter stick. If you play a lot of heavy rock, you may want a thicker, heavier stick with

def•i•ni•tion

A **rimshot** is when you hit the head and the rim of the drum simultaneously with the bead and shoulder of the drumstick.

a big, round bead. In either case, you still have dozens of different models to choose from; you might have to test a half-dozen different models to find the one that feels right to you.

That said, for good all-around drum set playing, it's hard to beat a 5A or 5B, which all stick manufacturers produce. For playing small-group jazz or in intimate surroundings, consider a 7A or 8A or something similar.

Hitting the Drums—and Cymbals

Once you have your drums and cymbals positioned, you can start playing. If you've never played a drum set before, this is easier said than done. That's because there are so many things involved—a large number of drums and cymbals to hit, as well as two pedals to play with your feet.

If you're first starting out, I recommend simplifying things at first. Practice playing with your hands only, playing a ride pattern on the ride cymbal and two-and-four backbeats on the snare. Once you get this coordination down, you can add two-and-four hi-hat "chicks" with your left foot, and then one-and-three bass drum pulses with your right foot. Concentrate on playing a steady beat; don't let yourself slow down when things get complicated.

> **Pro Tip**
>
> One of the best ways to practice keeping a steady beat is to practice with a metronome. This emulates the rock-steady *click track* drummers use when in a recording studio.

A drum set drummer typically uses the right hand to keep time on either the closed hi-hat or the ride cymbal. The time you keep depends on the song but is typically straight eighth notes (eight to a bar), straight quarter notes (four to a bar), or, if you're playing jazz or a shuffle beat, a "spang spang-a-lang spang-a-lang" kind of pattern.

While your right hand is keeping time, your left hand is playing backbeats (two and four) on the snare drum. Your left hand can also play other patterns—and even move around your toms—while your right hand continues to play steady time. Your hands work together only when you come to the end of a phrase and need to play a fill on your toms.

In terms of stroke, you should play the snare drum just as you would a concert snare, with a quick down-and-up lifting motion. Use a similar motion with the toms, although you may have to use a heavier stroke, especially with a low-pitched, loosely tightened head.

For the cymbals, play the ride cymbal with the bead of your stick, as you would a concert suspended cymbal. Play the crash cymbals with the shoulder of your stick against the cymbal edge. As for the hi-hat, playing with either the stick bead or shoulder is common, depending on the sound you want to create.

It's ergonomically correct to turn your body slightly as you move around the set. That said, you don't want to have to twist so much that playing the far left or the far right of your kit is uncomfortable. Not only is this physically bad for you; it will also slow you down. Ideally, you want your movement around your set to be as economical as possible. The less you have to move, the faster you can play!

Learning Basic Beats

We'll conclude this chapter with some basic and common drum set beats, for different types of music. In drum set notation, the lines and spaces of the percussion staff represent the different drums and cymbals of your kit, as shown in the following example.

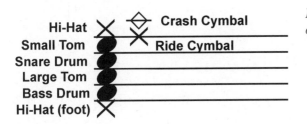

Notating the drums and cymbals of the drum set.

Basic Rock Beats

Most popular music today—rock, country, hip hop, you name it—is based on a straight-eighth-note beat with heavy backbeats on counts two and four. You can play various bass drum patterns against this beat, but it's all variations on a common theme.

The straight-eighth ride pattern in rock music can be played either on the hi-hat (typically closed or partially closed) or ride cymbal. You may want to change this up over the course of a song, playing the (softer) hi-hats during the verses and the (louder) ride cymbal during the choruses. But that's entirely up to you; unlike the more formally structured orchestral and marching playing, drum set playing is all about personal interpretation.

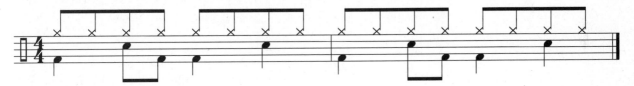

A common rock beat.

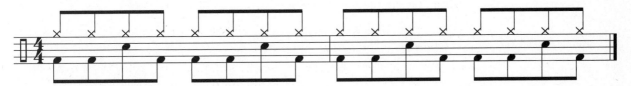

A variation on the basic rock beat.

Basic Shuffle Beats

Unlike the straight-eighth rock beat, the shuffle beat is based on an eight-note triplet pattern. It's more of a rolling beat, similar to the swing beat used in jazz music—but with a heavier backbeat.

A basic shuffle beat with a straight quarter-note ride pattern.

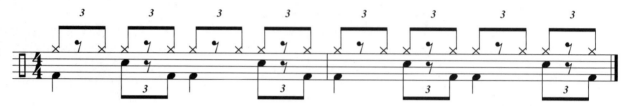

A more sophisticated shuffle beat with broken-triplet ride pattern.

Basic Jazz Beats

Grace Note

This difference in execution makes it almost impossible to notate the jazz feel. Some notation uses straight eighths to represent the swing, while another notation uses dotted eighths. I've opted for the triplet notation, and I'll let you determine how it's interpreted.

In this context, I'm defining jazz as music with a swing beat. While that doesn't cover all styles of jazz, it's a place to start.

The swing beat has more of a triplet feel than a straight-eighth feel—although that isn't always quite it, either. Some jazz has more of a dotted-eighth feel, while other tunes—typically up-tempo bop—are played with almost straight eighths, but kind of bounced. However, you play it, however, the swing beat needs to *swing*; it requires a lighter touch than with rock or shuffle playing.

The jazz beat is driven by the ride cymbal, using some variation of the "spang spang-a-lang spang-a-lang" pattern. The ride pattern is usually accompanied by a firm two-and-four "chick" with your left foot on the hi-hat. A constant two-and-four backbeat on the snare drum is less common, however; in much jazz drumming, your left hand is free to fill in the spaces extemporaneously on the snare drum.

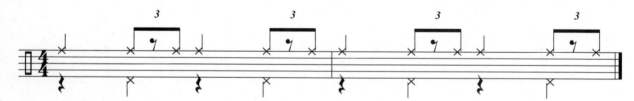

A simple swing beat, with just ride cymbal and hi-hat.

A more sophisticated jazz beat, with some fun play between the snare and bass drum.

Playing Fills

Most songs are made up of musical phrases. A phrase typically lasts for 4, 8, or 16 measures. Each new phrase begins a new musical idea—a new verse, sometimes, or a chorus.

To set up the new phrase properly, drummers are often called upon to play a fill to bridge the old phrase with the new. This fill is a short lead-in to the new phrase, typically using tom-toms or the snare, and generally lasting anywhere from one to four beats.

For example, if you're playing four-bar phrases, you might play a fill in the fourth measure, starting on the third or fourth beat. If you're playing longer phrases, you might start your fill on the first or second beat of the last measure of the phrase. Typically, the fill carries over onto the first beat of the new phrase, often with a cymbal crash.

Fills let you use all the different components of your drum set. The following figures show a couple of examples of what you might choose to play. Remember, fills are seldom notated but left to the discretion of the drummer.

A simple two-beat fill.

A longer full-measure fill.

Using the Drum Sticks in Different Ways

In normal drum set playing, the basic stroke puts the bead of the stick in the exact center of the drum. There are other ways to use the stick, however, to create different sounds.

A Softer Backbeat with Rimclicks

On some soft songs, a heavy backbeat on the snare drum may be overkill. For a softer sound, try playing a *rimclick* instead.

Heads Up

You can also play a rimclick with the butt of the stick on the snare head, but you won't get the same wooden ring as you do with the bead on the head.

You play a rimclick by turning your left stick around so that you're holding on to the top end, not the butt. Now place the bead (which should be near the palm of your hand) on the head of the snare drum, slightly off-center. Raise the butt of the stick off the drum, and then bring it down on the opposite rim for a soft "click" sound.

You can vary the tone of a rimclick by changing where you place the bead of the stick on the head—and where on the stick you click against the rim. If you choke up on the stick, your rimclick will sound dry and constrained. It's better to find a position that produces optimum ring for a very open and woody sound.

Playing a rimclick on the snare drum.

A Louder Backbeat with Rimshots

For a more pronounced backbeat or a louder snare drum accent, try playing a *rimshot*. You play a rimshot by hitting the head of the drum and the rim simultaneously; the sound is part normal snare and part loud, woody accent.

Some drummers play rimshots on every backbeat—and angle their snare drums slightly forward to make it easier to hit every rimshot.

Play louder accents by using rimshots.

Pro Tip

If you play traditional grip, you can also play a rimshot by pressing the left stick down into the snare head and then hitting the left stick with the right stick. This is a common technique among jazz drummers.

Beyond Sticks: Playing with Brushes

If you play a lot of jazz—or a lot of soft ballads—you need to learn how to play with brushes. Brushes incorporate a "fan" of steel or plastic bristles, typically retractable, and are usually housed in a rubber-covered handle. When you hit a drum with a brush, the sound is softer and more diffused than when you hit it with a stick. And you can do more than just hit with a brush; you can drag it across the drumhead to make a steady swishing noise.

A pair of retractable brushes, with rubber handles.

(Photo courtesy of Pro-Mark.)

Jazz brush technique is all about moving the brush around the (coated) snare drumhead in a smooth, sustained motion. The typical approach is to set up a steady swishing movement with one hand while the other hand swishes around the head in a complementary or contrasting pattern and rhythm. The swish provides the "background noise" that would otherwise be provided by a ride cymbal or hi-hat.

The best way to approach the swishing movement is to think of "pushing" the brush into and around the head, making shapes. (Jazzers sometimes call this "stirring soup.") You push your left and right hands separately, each in its own pattern. You can use numerous patterns, but the easiest is to work each hand in its own separate circle.

Of course, it's important that your circling motion be done in time with the music. That is, you want the brush to be at the same place on the head on every downbeat. You might complete one full circle in the space of a single quarter-note beat. Start at the top of the circle on one, and return to the top (and get ready to go again) on two. You should strive to make the resulting sound as smooth and consistent as possible.

Pro Tip
For proper jazz brush technique, you need a drumhead with a rough surface. Today's coated batter heads try to replicate the rough surface of the original calfskin heads.

Grace Note _____

There is no hard-and-fast rule for how to play brush patterns. You can swish with either hand, using any number of circular and noncircular patterns, as long as you produce the proper sound.

Reading a Drum Chart

Playing the drum set is always fun, and often challenging. That's because you don't always have notated music in front of you.

That's right, in many playing situations you don't get any music to read. If there's no chart available (which is common when playing casual gigs with rock and country bands), you're left to figure out the song's structure all by yourself. This requires good ears, good communication with the other band members, and a basic familiarity with the songs being played.

In other cases, however, you'll receive a written drum chart. Not all charts are alike, however.

Some drum charts are quite detailed, with the notes for each drum and cymbal written out measure by measure. This is rare, however; most charts just indicate a basic beat or feel, and tell you how many measures to play in each section of the song. You're left to interpret the chart in your own unique style.

That said, even the simplest chart typically includes specific notation for big accents or important parts of the song. You might see a measure of accented notes, or an indication to lay out for a bar or two. Think of these markings as road signs along the roadway; they provide guidance as you navigate through the song. Just remember to count through the measures as best you can, and play (or don't) the notated sections as they come up.

The Least You Need to Know

- The drum set is composed of a snare drum, bass drum, two or more tom-toms, and a variety of cymbals—hi-hats, rides, and crashes.

- Playing the drum set is much more involved than simple snare drum playing; you have to coordinate all four limbs across multiple drums and cymbals.

- Rock beats are based on a straight-eighth-note pulse with a two-and-four snare drum backbeat.

- Shuffle beats are based on an eighth-note triplet pulse.

- Jazz and swing beats are based on a "spang spang-a-lang" ride pattern—with no snare drum backbeat.

- You don't have to play drums with sticks; you can also use brushes on the snare drum.

Drum Circle Drums and Percussion

In This Chapter

◆ What a drum circle is—and who plays in it

◆ Drums of the drum circle

◆ World percussion in the drum circle

Our look at "popular" percussion concludes with those instruments used in drum circles. These are typically native or "folk" instruments—hand drums, shakers, and the like. They're often played by amateur drummers, regular folks who are more interested in the communal experience than in technically mastering the instruments.

Understanding the Drum Circle

What exactly is a drum circle? As the name implies, a drum circle is a group of people gathered in a circle to play drums and other percussion instruments. While that explanation is somewhat circular (as is the drum circle itself!), it's also apt; gather three or more people, hand them each something to hit or shake, and you have a rudimentary drum circle.

Here's what a drum circle is *not*. It's not a trained percussion ensemble playing a prepared piece of music. It's not a drumming class led by a teacher. It's not a group of professional musicians gathering together in any formal setting.

A drum circle is something much less formal—more like an extended jam session than anything else. There is no written music to perform; everyone kind of does his or her own thing. The jams can last from several minutes to an hour or more. The point is not to make great music, but rather to enrich one's personal experience through the music. It's more about recreation than performance.

The whole notion of drum circles started in the 1960s, as kind of a counter-cultural idea. Drum circles remain a bit countercultural today, with a bit of a hippie feel about them. Not that there's anything wrong with that; playing drums together is actually a great way to get in touch with oneself and one's fellow humans.

Grace Note

The countercultural underpinnings of today's drum circles are betrayed by a chief drum circle spokesperson, Grateful Dead drummer Mickey Hart. Here's what he said about drum circles in a 1991 testimony before the United States Senate Special Committee on Aging:

"The drum circle offers equality because there is no head or tail. It includes people of all ages. The main objective is to share rhythm and get in touch with each other and themselves. To form a group consciousness…(A) new voice, a collective voice, emerges from the group as they drum together."

A little touchy-feely and new-agey, to be sure, but an accurate enough description of the phenomenon.

We Don't Need No Stinking Rules!

Drum circles come in all types and sizes. They can range from a small handful of players to circles with thousands of participants. There is no upper or lower size limit.

Grace Note

Drum circles with no formal moderation are sometimes called *anarchic drum circles*.

Nor are there limits as to where the drum circle takes place, or how it unfolds. You can host a drum circle in your living room, at your local church or community center, in the middle of a big park, or at an amphitheater or concert hall. The drum circle can be free-form, with no designated leader, or it can be hosted by a facilitator who acts as kind of like a bandleader or conductor. Again, there are no formal rules.

Even facilitated drum circles are rather free-form in nature. The facilitator guides and encourages the participants, but his role stops there; there's no formal directing of the musicians, no right or wrong in terms of who plays what and when. The focus is on the connection and communication among participants.

Some drum circles are ethno-specific (meaning they focus on music of a specific culture), some are designed for meditation, some have healing goals, some are more spiritual, and some are described as "thunder" circles, which are unfacilitated, free-form jams. There are community drum circles, for celebration and connecting socially; corporate drum circles, to build teamwork and morale; diversity drum circles, to build unity and appreciate ethnic differences; and recreational drum circles, purely for the enjoyment of playing together. All I know is that drum circles can be rewarding in a lot of different ways—and they're a lot of fun.

Who Drums—and Why?

Drum circles include individuals from all walks of life. Some are amateur musicians, some played music when they were younger but trailed away over time, others still play in some fashion today. Most participants, however, are not professional musicians. A typical drum circle includes young people and old people, white-collar professionals and blue-collar workers, college students and retirees. Anyone can join, and you'll meet a wide variety of people if you decide to do so. After all, circle drumming is a social activity as well as a musical one.

Why do all these different types of people participate in drum circles? After all, it's not a formal performing situation. In fact, most drum circles have few if any professional percussionists as members.

For some participants, playing in a drum circle is purely a recreational activity, a way to let off steam and have a little fun. For others, it's a social or cultural thing, a way to get in touch with different (musical) cultures. For others, it's a truly musical activity, a place to practice drumming as a hobby. For still others, it's a way to meet new people. Whatever works for you.

Why Drums?

As to the question of why *drum* circles (as opposed to woodwind circles or keyboard circles), it's a matter of expediency. Not to offend all the trained percussionists reading this book, but it's a lot easier to hit a drum than it is to play an arpeggio on a clarinet or a chord on a piano. Drums were the first percussion instruments for a reason, and that reason holds today: They're easy for anyone to pick up and play, even just a little.

In addition, it helps to remember that drums are used by cultures all around the world. Societies use drums to celebrate and communicate; it makes sense to use this universal family of instruments to unite people within a recreational drum circle.

A drum circle in Asheville, North Carolina—djembes, ashikos, djundjuns, and a guy dancing in the middle.

(Photo courtesy of Jason Sandford under the Creative Commons 2.0 license.)

Drums of the Drum Circle

You won't find marimbas and timpani in a drum circle. Drum circles are all about easy-to-play hand drums and percussion. Nothing that has a steep learning curve; you want the average participant to be able to sit down and start playing without a lot of instruction necessary.

So what types of drums are most common in drum circles? Here's a short list:

♦ **Djembe.** The djembe is a traditional African hand drum and often the lead drum in a drum circle. The djembe can produce three primary notes: the bass, the tone, and the slap. Drum-circle rhythms often revolve around two or three different djembe parts, each with a different pattern of the three basic notes.

♦ **Ashiko.** A popular alternative to the djembe, the ashiko is a similar single-headed African drum but with a slightly lower tone. It produces the same three primary notes.

♦ **Doumbek.** A goblet-shaped hand drum from the Middle East, which produces a mix of crisp high tones and deep bass tones.

♦ **Bongos.** These are small instruments of Cuban ancestry, producing a higher-pitched snap than the larger African instruments. A set of bongos has two drums attached to each other.

♦ **Congas.** These are also traditional Cuban instruments, larger than bongos, that require a more practiced technique to produce various tones. While professional players often play multiple conga drums, it's more typically one drum per player in a drum circle.

♦ **Djun-djun.** This is the traditional bass drum of the drum circle, typically played with wooden sticks or padded mallets.

♦ **Surdo.** Another bass drum in the circle, this one from Brazil.

♦ **Ewe drums.** This family of drums from Ghana is played with sticks, and includes the *sogo*, *kagan*, and *boba* drums.

In short, hand drums are the common currency of the drum circle—and African hand drums the currency of choice. It doesn't matter whether it's a big drum or a little one, as long as you can strike it with the hand without having to learn much in the way of playing technique. (This is why the djembe is more common than the conga; conga drums require more technical skills to play properly.)

And these aren't the only drums you'll find. Many drum circles incorporate a variety of handmade frame drums and auxiliary percussion instruments. What you don't find, in most instances, is a full drum set, which would tend to overpower the lower-volume hand drums in the circle. Stick with hand drums and ethnic drums, and you'll fit right in.

Grace Note

Learn more about bongos, congas, and surdos in Chapter 12. Learn more about the djembe, ashiko, djun-djun, and Ewe drums in Chapter 13. And learn about doumbeks and related drums in Chapter 14.

Hand Percussion of the Drum Circle

Drum circles incorporate more than just drums, however. Any type of small percussion instrument can fit in, whether shaken or struck.

The most common hand-percussion instruments found in drum circles today include the following:

- ◆ **Tambourine.** Perhaps the most common hand-percussion instrument in drum circle circles, it's easy to shake out a beat or hit against your hand for accents. Headless models are most common.

- ◆ **Shakers.** All types of shakers are used to create the background beat—African shekeres, Latin American maracas, non-denominational cylindrical shakers, you name it.

- ◆ **Bells.** We're talking variations of the Latin American cowbell, including the African gankogui, the two-tone agogo bell, and the like.

- ◆ **Claves and woodblocks.** Just as metal bells are used to provide specific rhythms, so are wooden instruments, specifically the clave and woodblock.

- ◆ **Scrapers.** These instruments are scraped to create a scratchy type of rhythm. The guiro is probably the most common scraper among circle drummers, but other similar instruments are also popular.

Drum circles can also include all manner of homemade, hand-percussion instruments. Handmade shakers are probably the most common; you can get an acceptable sound by tossing some small pebbles into an empty two-liter soda bottle, for example. In any instance, if it makes a noise when you shake it or strike it, you can play it in just about any drum circle!

Rhythms of the Drum Circle

With all these different instruments, just what kind of music can you expect in a drum circle?

First of all, don't expect anything written; most drum circle music is totally improvised. That doesn't mean, however, that it's a total free for all.

The way it works is that a facilitator or lead drummer will start things off by playing a common rhythm on a single instrument. This may be a clave rhythm on a bass instrument, like a surdo or djun-djun, or something equally recognizable on a djembe or doumbek. Once this foundation gets established, other drummers chime in with other repeating rhythms. It builds from there.

It might take several minutes for the whole thing to get cooking, but cooking it gets. You might even find one or more drummers doing a solo thing on top of the rhythmic foundation, but that's not necessary. Remember, the drum circle is a collective enterprise, not a showcase for soloists. It's all about everybody contributing to the groove.

The Least You Need to Know

- ◆ A drum circle is a group of typically non-professional musicians playing drums and hand-percussion instruments.

- ◆ Hand drums, such as djembes and congas, are the most popular instruments in most drum circles.

- ◆ Hand-percussion instruments, such as shakers and tambourines, are also popular.

Part 5

The World of Ethnic Percussion

Congas and tablas and djembes, oh my! The world of percussion encompasses the entire world—not just traditional Western music. There are some very cool instruments found in Latin American, African, Middle Eastern, Indian, and Asian music, and you need to know at least a little bit about all of them.

Chapter 12

Latin Percussion

In This Chapter

◆ Learning the history of Latin American and Caribbean music

◆ Discovering bongos, congas, timbales, and other Latin drums

◆ Getting to know Latin hand percussion

◆ Introducing the Caribbean steel drum

Our tour of world percussion starts just south of the U.S. border. Interesting and unique Latin percussion instruments come from just about every country in Central and South America, as well as the islands of the Caribbean. Given the close proximity of these cultures, it's no surprise that Latin percussion has infiltrated Western popular culture—as well as our marching and orchestral music.

Although we tend to think of and use Latin percussion instruments as auxiliary percussion, that's not the case in Latin America and the Caribbean, where the instruments originated. In pure Latin music, many of these percussion instruments are likely to be more prominent than the drum set!

Understanding Latin and Caribbean Music

Latin percussion instruments evolved out of the local music of Latin America and the Caribbean, which is itself a mix of native styles and styles that crossed over from Africa with the slave trade. This blend makes Latin and Caribbean music some of the most interesting music anywhere in the world—more rhythmic than other Western music, with a great deal of variety from country to country—and region to region.

Caribbean Music

The music of the Caribbean is really the music of individual islands. Each island in the area has its own native flavor and history, with the entire region informed by European and (primarily) African influences.

The history of Caribbean music is tied up in the history of the Caribbean itself. That history is one of a native land invaded by outsiders; the entire region was colonized as part of the Spanish, French, English, and Danish empires. This colonial influence helped to erode the native culture; further erosion occurred when the Europeans imported African slaves to work the sugar and coffee plantations on their island colonies. In many cases, the native cultures—and the native musics—were replaced with those brought over from Africa.

At this point, whatever common Caribbean culture existed was splintered. Each of the European powers carved out their own cultures on their respective islands. Even with the ending of the colonial period, this is the Caribbean we have today—a series of subtly different cultures from island to island.

This island-specific culture also informs the music of the Caribbean. Every island has its distinct musical styles, all inspired, to one degree or another, by the music brought over from the African slaves. As such, most Caribbean music, however unique to its own island culture, includes elements of African music—heavy use of percussion instruments, complex rhythmic patterns, and call and response vocals.

The most popular Caribbean musical styles include calypso and soca, from Trinidad and Tobago; ska and reggae, from Jamaica; and salsa, mamba, and rumba, from Cuba. Caribbean percussion instruments include congas, bongos, timbales, various types of cowbells, and the steel drums of Trinidad.

Central and South American Music

Central and South America—the areas from Mexico on south that we collectively call Latin America—are just as diverse, musically, as the islands of the Caribbean.

Like Caribbean music, the music of native Latin Americans was all but obliterated by the influx of European culture when Spain and Portugal colonized the region. This led to the infusion of European string and wind instruments to the native musical culture. In addition, some African rhythms and vocal styles became native, thanks to the African slave trade.

Also like the Caribbean, every region in Latin America has its own unique musical heritage. Some of the best-known musical styles include the samba and bossa nova, from Brazil; the merengue from the Dominican Republic; the tango from Argentina; and mariachi, ranchera, and Tejano (Tex-Mex) music from Mexico. Latin American percussion instruments include the surdo, repinique, caixa, tamborim, cajón, cuica, claves, guiro, castanets, cabasa, pandeiro, and maracas.

Discovering Latin Drums

Many Latin American and Caribbean drums are popular enough to be recognized by even nonmusicians in the United States. Most of these drums are hand drums, often used with other percussion instruments to create complex multi-instrument rhythmic patterns.

Conga

Probably the most well-known Latin percussion instrument is the *conga*, a deep, single-headed hand drum from Cuba. Congas can be constructed from the traditional wood or the more resilient fiberglass; heads are typically calfskin, although some drums use plastic heads.

Three wood-shelled conga drums from Latin Percussion.

(Photo courtesy of Latin Percussion.)

Like most Caribbean drums, congas are derived from similar African drums, in this case the Makuta drums from Central Africa, which were made from hollowed-out logs. Unlike the Makuta drums, however, congas are traditionally made from staves of wood, like a barrel—and, in fact, were thought to be originally made from salvaged barrels.

The conga's head is screw-tensioned. Tuning is done while playing the open tone (discussed shortly); when playing an open tone, the drum should ring loudly and with a clear tone. Tune the head too loose and it will sound dead and somewhat flappy. Tune the head too tight and it will sound pinched.

Heads Up

A loosely tuned head can also cause hand injuries, as you don't get the natural rebound you do with a tighter tensioning.

A conga player can play two or more congas of different sizes, either mounted on stands or positioned between the player's legs. Traditional sizes are 10 to 11 inches for the smallest drum (called the *quinto*), 11 to 12 inches for the standard drum (called the *conga*, of course), and 12 to 13 inches for the larger drum (called the *tumbadora* or *tumbao*).

Conga drums are essential to any Latin groove. You generate different sounds by hitting the head in different places and with different parts of your hand. Here are the most popular conga strokes and how to play them:

♦ **Open tone:** Creates a full, resonant sound. This is the standard stroke on the congas. Strike the drum between the center of the head and the rim with the full length of your fingers, just in from your palm. Let your fingers bounce off the head immediately after striking.

♦ **Slap:** Creates a broad ringing sound. This is used for loud accents, typically on the highest conga. A slap is played like an open tone but with your fingers slightly cupped. Use your fingertips to strike the drum with a hard flicking or whipping motion.

♦ **Closed slap:** Creates a less resonant accent. You produce a closed slap just like the regular (open) slap, but with your other hand pressing against the drum head to muffle it slightly.

♦ **Muted tone:** Creates a deep, somewhat muffled thud. Strike the drum gently with your entire hand, keeping your fingers closed. Your fingers should strike near the center of the head, the palm closer to the rim.

♦ **Light touch:** Produces a very light sound, useful for background time-keeping. Strike the head much like you do with the open tone, but with the palm of the hand resting on the drum and the fingers remaining on the head after the hit (instead of bouncing off).

♦ **Bass tone:** Typically played on the lowest conga, this produces a low resonant tone. Strike the drum dead center with the palm or heel of your hand. Let your hand bounce off the head immediately after striking.

Then there is the *tumbao* technique, typically played on the largest drum, the tumbao. This is an advanced Afro-Cuban technique, commonly used in salsa music, created by rocking between the heel (palm) and the fingertips of the left hand. When striking the palm, raise the fingers off the head; when striking the fingertips, raise the palm off the head.

Use this technique to play the tumbao pattern—a series of eighth notes with heel (H), fingertips (F), slap (S), and open tone (O) strokes.

Grace Note

The slap is sometimes called the *open slap*, to distinguish it from the more muffled closed slap.

How to play the six basic conga strokes.

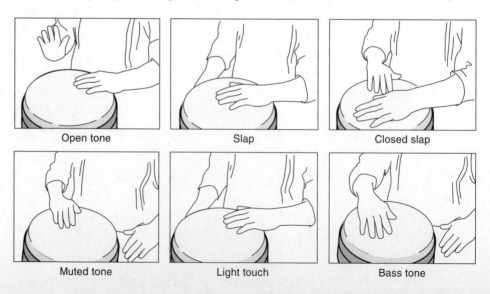

Open tone | Slap | Closed slap

Muted tone | Light touch | Bass tone

Playing the tumbao conga pattern.

L L R L L L R R
H F S F H F O O

Bongos

Bongos are, in a way, like small congas. Like congas, bongos hail from Cuba and are played with your hands and fingers. Unlike congas, which are singular drums with very deep shells, bongos are shallow drums that come in pairs (a small one and a large one joined together by a bridge).

Bongos are single-headed drums that create a higher-pitched tone than do conga drums. Most bongos are made from wood shells with calfskin heads, although some models have fiberglass shells and plastic heads. Bongos are typically available in 6- and 7-inch or 7- and 8-inch pairs.

Latin Percussion calfskin bongos.

(Photo courtesy of Latin Percussion.)

Traditionally, bongos are played sitting down, held between your knees, although in an orchestral or popular music environment, it's not uncommon to see bongos mounted on a stand for easier access. In the traditional position, sit at the edge of the seat with your back straight and your forearms resting on your thighs. The bongos should be positioned between your legs, with the smaller drum on your left. Angle the drums downward slightly, away from you; this makes it easier to hit the rim of the instrument.

Grace Note

The larger bongo is called the *hembra;* the smaller drum is called the *macho.*

You play bongos in pretty much the same way you play congas, using your hands and fingers to get different sounds from the drums. The big difference is that you primarily use your fingers rather than your entire hand, due in part to the smaller size of the bongo heads.

There are six basic strokes, similar to the conga strokes:

◆ **Open tone:** Produces a loud, ringing sound. Hit near the edge of the head with the inside knuckles of your fingers, then let your fingers bounce off the head.

- ◆ **Slap:** Produces a loud popping sound. The slap is used primarily for accents. Cup your fingers slightly and use the tips of your fingers to strike the drum with a hard, flicking motion.

- ◆ **Closed slap:** Creates a less resonant accent. You produce a closed slap just like the regular (open) slap, but with the thumb of the opposite hand pressing against the drumhead to muffle it slightly.

- ◆ **Rim shot:** Creates a very loud accent. Snap your fingers off the edge of the head.

- ◆ **Heel-tip:** Produces a subtle sound ideally suited for background time-keeping. Rest your hand on the head and rock from the heel of your hand to your fingers, as you do with the conga tumbao pattern. Your hand should remain in constant contact with the head.

- ◆ **Muted tone:** Creates a soft, muffled sound. Strike the drum with the inside knuckles of your fingers, as with the open tone stroke, but let your fingers rest on the head after the hit; don't let them rebound off the head.

The basic bongo pattern in Latin music is called the *martillo* or "hammer." It's played with a combination of open tone (O), closed slap (S), and muted tones (M).

The martillo bongo pattern.

```
R L R L R L R L
S M M M S M O M
```

Timbales

Timbales are a pair of shallow single-headed drums tuned to different (indefinite) pitches. Unlike congas and bongos, timbales are not hand drums; they're primarily played with sticks—although you can play some ghost notes with your hand.

The drums themselves are steel or brass with either calf or plastic heads. A typical set of timbales has one 14-inch diameter drum, called the *macho*, and one 15-inch diameter drum, called the *hembra*; the larger drum is placed to the player's left. Timbale sticks are thinner than normal drumsticks, more like wooden dowels, with two butt ends and no bead.

Traditional tuning puts timbale heads at a low- to mid-range tension—not overly tight. This creates a tone that is somewhat deeper than you might expect—in fact, timbales were originally designed to replace traditional timpani in early twentieth-century Cuban orchestras. The two drums should be tuned about a fourth or fifth apart.

Timbales are typically used both to create a constant rhythm and to provide accents and solo parts. Many timbale players play the shells of the drums as well as the heads, and typically use one or more cowbells, woodblocks, and cymbals, in conjunction with the timbales.

Tito Puente model timbales from Latin Percussion.

(Photo courtesy of Latin Percussion.)

For example, the following pattern fuses an accented syncopated rhythm (called the *cáscara* or *paila*) played on the shell of the high timbale with a clave pattern played on the head of the low drum.

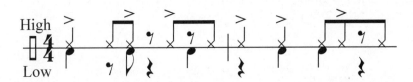

A typical two-drum timbale pattern; the top notes are played on the shell of the high timbale.

Because of the variety of possible sounds available, the timbale player is the master drummer in authentic Cuban music. As such, a player must develop an extensive vocabulary of sounds, techniques, and rhythms. It's not just about simple rhythmic accompaniment; a flashy timbale solo is often a featured part of many songs. It's a fun instrument to play, but a demanding one to learn.

Surdo

The *surdo* provides the bass voice in much Brazilian music, including and especially the samba. It's also a popular instrument among the drum circle crowd.

The modern surdo is evolved from the atabaque family of African drums. The instrument itself is a large, double-headed drum, slightly resembling the large tom in a modern drum set. The surdo is traditionally made from wood, but metal versions are also common. Heads can be either calfskin or plastic, anywhere from 18 to 22 inches in diameter—although larger sizes are also common. The drum can be either mounted on legs or carried on a shoulder strap. When using a strap, the drum is slung rather low—below waist level.

Grace Note

Some music requires the use of multiple surdos, each tuned to a different (indefinite) pitch, to create intricate bass parts.

Surdos with leg mounts and shoulder straps from Pearl.

(Photo courtesy of Pearl Drums.)

You play the surdo with a single mallet, similar to a bass drum mallet, typically held in your right hand. You can then mute the batter head with your left hand. This enables a variety of different tones: right mallet open, left hand open, left hand muted (striking into and pressing the head), and right mallet muted (with the left hand pressed against the head). When you press your left hand into the head, this also raises the pitch of any following notes.

Position the surdo below waist level and play with a single mallet.

In some Brazilian music, multiple surdos of different sizes are employed. The *primeira* (first) part is played by the largest, deepest surdo, and provides the pulse for the section. The second part is played by the slightly smaller *segunda* or *resposta* surdo, while the smallest surdo plays the higher *terceira* part.

A samba rhythm played on three surdos.

Repinique

The *repinique* is another double-headed Brazilian drum. It has a metal shell with heads of either 10 or 12 inches in diameter. The instrument is typically tuned extremely tight, the better to cut through the rest of the rhythm section.

A metal repinique complete with carrying strap.

(Photo courtesy of Pearl Drums.)

You play the repinique with two thin sticks, similar to timbale sticks. Alternatively, you can play the instrument with one stick and one hand. The drum is typically suspended on a shoulder strap; you play the top head only.

Repinique parts are similar to snare drum parts in marching music. Instead of playing a fixed rhythm, as with most other Latin instruments, the repinique typically plays a more linear, fluid part with lots of rolls, syncopation, and accents.

Caixa

The *caixa* (pronounced "ka-sha") is a Brazilian snare drum. It looks and sounds similar to a standard orchestral or drum set snare drum. The drum typically is 6 inches or more deep with a 12-inch diameter head. Tuning is very tight, the better to enable the use of buzz rolls, as is common when playing the samba.

You play the caixa with drumsticks, using either traditional or matched grip. Unlike the Western snare drum, the caixa is played with the snare side up, so you have to take care to avoid hitting the snares themselves.

Traditionally, the caixa was held on the shoulder. (And still played with two sticks!) Today, the caixa is more likely to be attached to a shoulder strap and played like an old-school marching snare drum.

Like the repinique, the caixa plays the snare drum role in the Brazilian drum section. Expect lots of fast sixteenth notes, rolls, accents, and syncopation, and part that varies from measure to measure.

The caixa, a Brazilian snare drum.

(Photo courtesy of Latin Percussion.)

Cajón

The *cajón* is a Peruvian instrument, a kind of box drum that sounds a low bass note. It literally looks like a box, constructed from sheets of wood.

Five of the six sides of the box are made from thick sheets of wood. The sixth side is thin plywood and acts as the "head" or striking surface; the opposite wood side has a round sounding hole cut into it.

To play the cajón, sit on top of the box with the plywood "head" between your knees. Strike the plywood side with the fingers and palms of your hand.

An LP cajón; the sound hole is on the opposite side.

(Photo courtesy of Latin Percussion.)

Tamborim

The *tamborim* is a small, single-headed frame drum, no jingles, typically about 6 inches in diameter. You hold the tamborim in one hand and play it with a thin wooden stick held in the other. Alternately, you can strike the tamborim with a bundle of wooden or plastic rods, which creates a softer, flamlike sound.

There's a special technique involved in just holding the tamborim. Place your thumb over the top of the head and your fingers on the inside of the head. This way you can mute the head with either your thumb or fingers, or use your middle finger to play ghost or filler notes against the inside of the head.

The tamborim—a small frame drum.

(Photo courtesy of Pearl Drums.)

You typically play highly syncopated rhythms on the tamborim, alternating open and muted notes. A talented player will fill in the holes in the syncopation with ghost notes on the inside of the drum.

A syncopated tamborim rhythm, with both open (○) and muted (+) notes.

Cuica

The *cuica* is an interesting instrument, actually a type of friction drum that isn't hit with your hand or a stick. It's a single-headed metal drum, 6 to 10 inches in diameter, with a small wooden dowel attached to (and through) the underside of the goatskin head. By manipulating this dowel, a variety of different squeaks and groans are created. It sounds more like a wild animal than a typical drum!

The cuica—note the end of the inside dowel sticking through the head.

(Photo courtesy of Pearl Drums.)

You play the cuica by holding it under one arm, your left hand resting on the head and your right arm inserted into the open end of the drum. Use your right hand to rub a wet cloth up and down the wooden dowel while using the thumb of your left hand to press down on the head near where the dowel is attached.

The rubbing motion creates the sound while your thumb raises or lowers the basic pitch.

There are two basic cuica strokes—pulling and pushing. The pulling stroke occurs when you pull your hand (and the dowel) down, towards you; the pushing stroke occurs when you push your hand (and the dowel) up, towards the head.

A typical cuica rhythm—pull down on the down arrows, and push up on the up arrows.

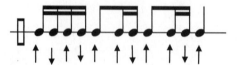

Playing Auxiliary Latin Percussion Instruments

Drums aren't the only instruments used in Latin percussion. There are also a variety of bells, blocks, and gourds that are hit, shaken, or even scraped.

Cowbell

The so-called *cowbell*, actually just a bell, is a staple of Latin American and Caribbean music. The typical cowbell is a medium-sized metal bell with one open end; various sizes are available with their own unique tonal characteristics.

A typical metal cowbell.

(Photo courtesy of Latin Percussion.)

The cowbell produces an indefinite pitch and very slight sustain. You play it with a wooden beater or drumstick, holding the cowbell in one hand and striking it with the back end of a drumstick held in the other. To produce a more ringing sound, strike near the open end. To produce a higher-pitched, more muffled sound, strike it near the closed end. To muffle all ringing, grasp the body of the cowbell tightly with your hand while holding it.

You can also mount one or more cowbells on a holder, which is common with timbale and drum set players. The cowbell is typically used to play a constant rhythm, like the clave (discussed in a moment), behind the rest of the percussion section.

A typically syncopated cowbell rhythm.

Agogo Bells

Agogo bells are a set of two pitched bells, kind of like small cowbells, connected via a curved piece of metal. One bell is smaller than another, so that each bell sounds its own unique (indefinite) pitch.

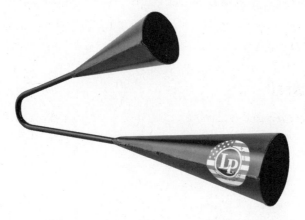

A set of agogo bells.

(Photo courtesy of Latin Percussion.)

You play agogo bells as if you're playing twin cowbells, hitting the instrument with a drumstick or metal beater. Agogo bells typically have a long ring, but you can muffle either bell with your hand if you want a less resonant sound.

A samba rhythm for the agogo bells.

Claves

Claves came to Latin America via Africa. They're essentially two wooden cylinders that are struck together to produce a highly resonant "click" sound.

That said, you can't just grab the two claves and knock them together; by gripping each clave tightly, you'll muffle any natural resonance and produce a sound that doesn't project well. Instead, you want to rest one clave in the palm of your hand and then strike it with the second gripped clave.

Start by making a fist from your left hand, then turn the fist palm up. Rest the clave lightly on your upturned knuckles, so that it's just setting there; if you turn your hand back over, the clave should fall to the ground. Now grab

Grace Note

The Latin clave rhythm evolved into the rock 'n' roll "Bo Diddley" beat popularized by, you guessed it, guitar legend Bo Diddley.

the second clave as you would a drumstick in your right hand. Strike the left-hand clave with the right-hand one, typically near the middle of the bar for best resonance.

Playing a pair of claves.

(Photo courtesy of Latin Percussion.)

Claves are typically used to play a repeating rhythm, also called the clave. The clave rhythm is a five-note, syncopated pattern played over two measures and should be familiar to listeners of both Latin American music and American popular music. The traditional clave is a 3/2 rhythm; it can also be reversed in a 2/3 pattern.

The 3/2 clave rhythm typically played on the claves.

The 2/3 clave rhythm—the traditional clave, reversed.

Guiro

The *guiro* is a unique scratched instrument. Traditionally, it's constructed from a cylindrical gourd with grooves cut around its circumference and two finger holes drilled into the bottom of the instrument. Modern guiros can be made from hollow metal or plastic, with some sort of handle attached.

Remo's traditional gourd guiro.

(Photo courtesy of Remo, Inc.)

To play the guiro, insert your thumb and first or second fingers into the finger holes, or just grasp the handle. Hold a thin wooden stick in your opposite hand and scrape it back and forth across the grooves to create the characteristic scratching sound.

Castanets

The *castanet* came to Latin America via Spanish colonists. It's a small hand-held instrument consisting of two wooden or plastic halves that are clicked together.

Traditional castanets are held in one hand and clicked together. More popular models are mounted to a handle (in both single-castanet and double-castanet configurations) for easier playing.

To play hand-held castanets, click the two halves together. To play handle-mounted castanets, whip the handle through the air until the two castanets click together. Optionally, you can strike the entire instrument against your leg to make the sound. In any case, the goal is absolute rhythmic clarity, which is challenging; it's easy to be sloppy on this particular instrument.

Traditional hand-held castanets.

(Photo courtesy of Latin Percussion.)

Cabasa

The *cabasa* is a type of shaker originally from Africa but adopted and adapted by Brazilian musicians over the years. The basic cabasa is a ribbed hollow gourd with strings of native beads around the outside. The more modern *afuche/cabasa* is a small, ribbed, metal cylinder covered by strings of metal beads.

Whichever type of cabasa you play, there are a number of different approaches to the instrument. First, you can use it as a standard shaker or rattle by holding the cabasa by the handle and shaking it with one hand. Second, you can hold the cabasa in one hand and strike it with the other, for a more percussive effect. And third, you can hold the cabasa in one hand and use the palm of your other hand to press the beads to the gourd/cylinder and then move them back and forth. This can also be accomplished by holding the beads in place with your second hand and then rotating the cabasa by the handle with your first hand.

A traditional gourd cabasa

(Photo courtesy of Latin Percussion.)

The popular modern afuche/ cabasa.

(Photo courtesy of Latin Percussion.)

Like all shakers, the characteristic rhythm of the cabasa is a steady quarter-, eighth-, or sixteenth-note background pattern.

Maracas

 Maracas are probably the most recognized Latin American shaker instrument. The instrument is traditionally constructed from a gourd with dried seeds inside and a handle attached; modern maracas may be made from hollow plastic with small plastic or metal balls inside.

A pair of maracas.

(Photo courtesy of Latin Percussion.)

Maracas are typically played in pairs, either one in each hand or two in a single hand. You shake the maracas forward and back with a sharp flick of your wrist to produce a steady quarter- or eighth-note rhythm. In most instances, you shake the two maracas together; for faster passages, however, you can hold one in each hand and alternate strokes.

Grace Note _____

Maracas are just one of many different shakers used in Latin and Afro-Cuban music. Other shakers are created from hollowed-out cylindrical gourds, or from hollow metal tubes, with dried seeds or small metal beads inside.

Pandeiro

The *pandeiro* is essentially a Brazilian tambourine. The construction is similar to the tambourine used in Western orchestral and popular music, but with heavier metal jingles. These jingles are mounted convex to each other, as opposed to the concave mounting on the Western tambourine.

The pandeiro—the Brazilian tambourine.

(Photo courtesy of Latin Percussion.)

The different jingles create a dryer sound than with the orchestral tambourine and allow for more subtlety in play. This is facilitated by a mix of open and closed tones in the supporting hand and various finger, thumb, and hand techniques in the playing hand.

One Last Thing: Steel Drums

There's one more drum, this one from the Caribbean, that bears discussion. This is the famous *steel drum*, also known as the *steelpan*, which originated on the island of Trinidad. The steel drum is unique in that it's a drum used to play melodies.

Indeed, a single steel drum can create an entire range of pitches. The "head" of the drum is actually a single sheet of metal, with different areas of the head hammer-tuned to different notes.

Each instrument is unique, as all steel drums are made by hand from an actual steel drum—that is, a 55-gallon oil barrel. One end of the barrel is cut off and discarded; the base or bowl of the opposite end is hammered into a series of pitches. Steel drums are available in various sizes and pitch ranges, from the low-pitched bass pan to the higher-pitched tenor or lead pan, used to play melodies.

Grace Note _____

Steel-drum players are called *pannists*. They play the drums using mallets constructed from wooden or aluminum handles with black surgical tubing wrapped around the head end.

Playing a set of steel drums.

(Photo courtesy of Flickr member _e.t under the Creative Commons 2.0 license.)

Since all steel drums are unique, the arrangement of the notes on the bowl differs from drum to drum. That's why the drums have the pitches written on each of the corresponding areas of the bowl; otherwise, you wouldn't know where to hit for what pitch.

The range of each drum varies by type; the deeper the drum, the smaller the range. The tenor pan, for example, has a range of three octaves, with the third starting at middle C and going up to a high E. The bass pan, in contrast, has only a four-note range, as each playing area is rather large to produce the bass-range notes.

Since most percussionists will not be called to play the steel drums, I'll stop this discussion here. Know that the steel drum is a unique instrument with a uniquely pleasing sound and warrants dedicated study if you wish to play it seriously.

The Least You Need to Know

- Latin American and Caribbean music and percussion instruments derive from a combination of native regional music, European colonial influences, and music and instruments brought to the New World by African slaves.

- Popular Latin American drums include the bongos, congas, timbales, and surdo.

- Popular Latin American hand percussion includes the cowbell, claves, maracas, guiro, and castanets.

- Also worth noting are steel drums from the Caribbean, capable of producing chromatic melodies and harmonies on what was once a 55-gallon oil drum.

Chapter 13

African Percussion

In This Chapter

◆ Uncovering the roots of African music and percussion

◆ Discovering African drums

◆ Playing shakers and bells

◆ Uncovering melodic African percussion

Our tour of world percussion now crosses the Atlantic Ocean to the big continent of Africa. This is where most Western percussion—as well as most Western music—originated, so there are lots of important and interesting instruments to examine.

Understanding African Music

In many ways, music is more important to African society than it is to Western society. In the West, music is a luxury or entertainment; in Africa, it is an integral part of everyday life.

Africans embrace music into their lives at an early age, often making their own musical instruments by the age of three or four. Children play musical games, and are capable of dancing to and playing very complex rhythms.

Music has ceremonial, ritual, and social functions in African culture. Important stages of a person's life are often marked by and celebrated with music. There are lullabies for babies, game songs for children, and music for adolescent initiation rites, weddings, funerals, and the like. And, not surprisingly, this ritualistic music is often accompanied by equally ritualistic dance.

While music is important to all African cultures, the type of music played differs significantly from culture to culture. We tend to think of Africa as a single consolidated place, but it's really a very large continent (second largest, after Asia) that contains four dozen independent countries and untold thousands of different tribes and cultures. Not surprisingly, then, the music of Africa is as varied as the continent's many nations, regions, and ethnic groups. But while there is no single pan-African music, there are shared characteristics in the music of different regions.

What does African music sound like? Well, like the music of Asia, India, and the Middle East, it's a highly rhythmic music—which explains the prevalence of percussion instruments. Most African music is constructed from complex rhythmic patterns, often involving one rhythm played against another to create a *polyrhythm*.

The most common African polyrhythm plays three beats on top of two, like a triplet played against straight notes—and it gets more complicated from that. As complex as this type of polyrhythm is to Western ears, it comes as naturally as breathing to the natives of Africa. It might take Western percussionists years to master these rhythms, but most little kids in Africa can play them without blinking twice. That's impressive.

Another facet of African music is that it's highly improvised. It works like this: The group itself plays a core rhythmic pattern, while a solo drummer improvises new patterns over the static original pattern. The result is spontaneous, yet familiar.

Discovering African Drums

The rhythmic nature of African music explains the large number and many types of drums and percussion instruments used. While many African drums are similar in construction and usage, the flora and culture of each region influences the construction of instruments in that region. For example, wooden drums are more popular in the forest regions of West Africa than in the treeless savanna areas of Southern Africa.

That said, many African drums are *goblet drums*, so-named because of their goblet shape. These are typically single-headed hand drums, with the top (head) wider than the bottom—just like a drinking goblet. You find goblet drums of various types all across the African continent, and even into the Middle East.

Djembe

One of the most well-known African goblet drums is the *djembe* (pronounced "JEM-bay"). The djembe is similar in sound and function to the Caribbean conga drum, but with a deeper bass note. Originating in the Mali Empire of West Africa, the djembe was originally used for ceremonial purposes and to motivate soldiers headed into battle, although it has much broader applications today.

The djembe—the most well-known African drum (to American audiences).

(Photo courtesy of Pearl Drums.)

As you might suspect, the djembe is shaped like a large goblet and covered by an animal skin (typically cow skin, goatskin, or antelope skin) head on the top. Most djembes are made by hand and thus vary in construction from drum to drum. The typical djembe is about 12 inches in diameter and 24 inches in height, although both smaller and larger drums are common. It's a versatile instrument, producing both thundering low notes and cracking high notes.

Grace Note

The djembe is particularly popular in drum circles. Learn more in Chapter 11.

You play the djembe with your bare hands in either a sitting position (the drum between your legs) or standing (with the drum attached to a shoulder strap). There are three primary notes you can create:

◆ **Tone:** Produces a round and full tone, more or less the standard note on the djembe. Hold your hand flat and firm, with the fingers tightly together. Strike near the rim with your fingers. The stroke should be quick, with your hand lifting off the head.

◆ **Slap:** Produces a sharp and resonant sound, perfect for accents. Relax your hand, with your fingers held loosely apart. Strike the rim of the drum with your knuckles and palm, allowing your fingertips to "slap" the head and immediately bounce off.

◆ **Bass:** Produces the lowest tone on the instrument, like a bass drum sound. Cup your hand slightly, with your middle knuckles raised just a bit. Strike near the center of the head with the palm and fingers of your hand, letting your slightly raised knuckles drop to the head. Remove your hand immediately after the stroke, as if the head were hot.

How to play the tone, slap, and bass notes on the djembe.

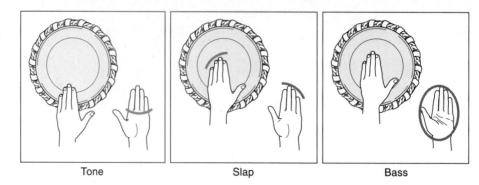

Tone Slap Bass

In larger African ensembles and drum circles, you're likely to find multiple djembes of different sizes playing two or three different parts. In this type of scenario, one or two supporting djembes will play a repeating interlocking polyrhythmic pattern, while the "solo" djembe will play a more fluid melodic rhythm.

A typical djembe rhythm; the lowest note is the bass, the middle the tone, and the top (×) the slap.

Ashiko

The *ashiko* is another goblet drum, similar to the djembe but with a slightly lower pitch. (Some consider the ashiko to be male and the djembe female.) It originated in Nigeria in West Africa. It is played throughout sub-Saharan Africa, as well as in American drum circles. A Cuban version of the ashiko is called the *boku*.

Like the djembe, the ashiko has three primary tones: the tone, the slap, and the bass. Playing technique and rhythms are similar to that of the djembe.

The ashiko—a "male" djembe.

(Photo courtesy of Remo, Inc.)

Batá

The *batá* is a two-headed Nigerian drum with one head larger than the other; the smaller head is called the *cha-cha* and the larger head is called the *enu*. The drum itself is hourglass-shaped and used primarily in religious ceremonies in both Africa and the Caribbean.

The batá is a tunable hand drum, available in three primary sizes. The *oconcolo* is the soprano batá, about 20 inches tall with 5- and 7-inch heads. The *itotele* is the alto or tenor drum, about 26 inches tall with 6- and 9-inch heads. The *iya* is the bass voice, about 27 inches tall with 7- and 12-inch heads.

A set of three batá drums from Latin Percussion.

(Photo courtesy of Latin Percussion.)

You play both heads of the batá. The instrument can be played in either a standing or sitting position. Standing, one or more batás are mounted horizontally on a stand. Sitting, lay a single instrument across the lap and place one hand on each head. You play the larger, enu, head with your dominant hand. The enu head has three primary tones: open tone, closed tone, and touch. The cha-cha head has two tones: slap and touch.

Given the complexities of four different tones on two different heads—and each hand playing independently from the other—batá music is challenging for Western drummers. Ideally, it should be learned under the guidance of a master native drummer.

Grace Note

The batá was introduced to Cuba by African slaves during the 1820s, and has since become an important instrument in that country's religious culture.

Djun-Djun

The *djun-djun* (also known as the *dundun* or *dunun*) is a two-headed bass drum typically used to accompany the djembe in West African drum ensembles. The drum is rope-tensioned with cow-skin heads.

There are three traditional sizes of djun-djuns: *kenkeni* (small—10-inch diameter head, 22 inches tall), *sangban* (medium—12-inch head, 24 inches tall), and *doundoumba* (large—14-inch head, 27 inches tall). Ensembles often use all three djun-djuns, each with its own musical role.

The traditional playing style lies the drum on its side, either on the floor or on a stand. You strike the head with a single stick; your other stick is used to strike a bell mounted on top of the djun-djun. The alternative *ballet style* stands three djun-djuns on the floor, with one person playing all three drums.

A Remo djun-djun.

(Photo courtesy of Remo, Inc.)

A typical djun-djun rhythm, accompanied by djun-djun bell (top line).

Udu

The *udu* is another popular Nigerian drum. This instrument is unique in that it's made from a clay pot with an extra hole in the side; there's no drumhead.

You play the instrument by hitting any part of the pot with your fingertips or the palm of your hand. You create a unique bass sound by hitting your hand against the big hole in the side.

Grace Note

By necessity, African instruments are constructed from materials common in a given region. This is why similar instruments vary in construction from region to region; different regions are host to different natural materials (trees, animals, and so on). The udu is one example of this, coming from a region without a lot of forests—but with an abundance of claylike dirt.

A clay udu drum.

(Photo courtesy of Latin Percussion.)

Talking Drum

African drums are nothing if not interesting. The most interesting of all, at least to my ears, are the *talking drums* of Nigeria. These drums—also known as *donno* or *luna*—are made to "talk" by varying the pitch of the drum. They're a type of pressure drum, where changing the pressure of the head changes the pitch.

The talking drum is an hourglass-shaped drum with two heads. The heads can be made from goatskin, lizard skin, or fish skin(!); multiple straps connect the two heads together. Different ethnic groups create talking drums of different sizes, ranging from 6 inches (head diameter) by 11 inches to 8 inches by 18 inches.

To play a talking drum, hold it under one arm and strike the head with a curved beater. Squeeze the tensioning cords with your arm to vary the pitch and make the drum "talk."

 Grace Note

Talking drums are used both for music and for communication. It is said that a complete talking drum language exists that can be used to transmit messages, signals, and, in some cases, even poetry.

In the Yoruban language, the talking drum is called the *dundun*—not to be confused with the *dundun* (*djun-djun*) bass drum.

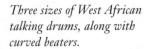

Three sizes of West African talking drums, along with curved beaters.

(Photo courtesy of Latin Percussion.)

Ngoma

In Central and Southern Africa, *ngoma* drums are common. These drums originated in the Congo and produce a sound similar to the conga drum.

The ngoma drum is a tall, single-headed drum, about 42 inches tall with an 11-inch or so animal-skin head; the bottom end is open. It can be played with hands or sticks.

A typical ngoma ensemble has four to seven drums, each with its own distinct musical role. You play the ngoma standing up with the drum tilted across the front of your body, secured by a waist strap.

A tall ngoma drum.

(Photo courtesy of DrummersTribe, www.drummerstribe.com.)

Ewe Drums

In Ghana, *Ewe* drums constitute an entire family of instruments. Ewe drumming ensembles include multiple drums of various types playing sophisticated cross-rhythms and polyrhythms.

Typical drums in an Ewe drumming ensemble include the following:

- **Kaganu.** The smallest drum and highest-pitched drum in the Ewe ensemble. It's about 18 inches long, with an open bottom.

- **Kroboto.** A squat, lower-pitched drum, about 20 inches long. Like the kaganu, the kroboto has an open bottom.

- ◆ **Kidi.** A mid-size drum with a wooden bottom, played with two wooden sticks.

- ◆ **Sogo.** A larger version of the kidi, played with either sticks or hands (or a combination of both).

- ◆ **Atsimevu.** The tallest of the Ewe drums—almost 4½ feet tall! It produces a mid-range bass sound when played with either two sticks or one hand and a stick. (The drum must be leaned over on a stand to be played.)

- ◆ **Boba.** The deepest-sounding drum in the Ewe ensemble, played like the atsimevu.

A set of Ewe drums—from left to right, the sogo, kroboto, atsimevu, kaganu, and kidi.

(Photo courtesy of African Drum Services, www.africandrumserivces. co.uk.)

Playing Other African Percussion Instruments

Aside from all the different types of drums, African percussion includes various shakers and bells. Let's look at a few.

Shekere

The *shekere* (pronounced "shek-ah-ray") is probably the most popular type of African shaker. The instrument is popular throughout most of the continent, and consists of a dried gourd surrounded by a net of beads.

Many small shekeres have handles to enable the instrument to be played with a single hand; larger instruments can be held in two hands. Like all shakers, you produce the characteristic sound by shaking the instrument in your hands.

Grace Note _____

Basket shakers are also popular in parts of Africa. These are constructed from small cane baskets with gourd bottoms; the pebbles inside produce sound when the instrument is shaken.

A Remo shekere.

(Photo courtesy of Remo, Inc.)

African Bells

Various types of metal bells are used throughout Africa to provide more color and rhythm to the music. The most common types of bells include the following:

- ◆ **Djun-djun bell.** Similar to a Latin American cowbell. This bell is typically attached to the side of a djun-djun drum and played with an iron striker.

- ◆ **Apiua bell.** A small iron bell about 6 inches long. It, too, is often attached to a djun-djun drum, although it can also be hand-held.

- ◆ **Gankogui.** The African ancestor of the Latin agogo bell. The instrument consists of a low bell (about 8 inches long) and a high bell (about 4 inches long), pitched about a third apart.

Melodic Percussion

Africa is also host to its own melodic percussion instruments—the native equivalents of the marimba and xylophone. These instruments include the larger *balafon* and smaller *gyil*, and are common in Northern Ghana and throughout Western Africa.

These African melodic instruments are made from wooden bars, suspended by leather straps on a wooden frame; the bars are all in a row, without the raised register found on the xylophone or marimba. In some instances, gourd resonators are placed under the bars. The typical balafon has between 17 and 21 bars; gyils are usually smaller, with no more than 14 bars.

Both the balafon and the gyil are typically tuned to the pentatonic scale. A common tuning is E♭ pentatonic: E♭, F, G, B♭, and C.

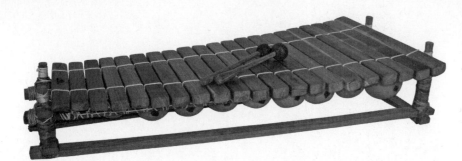

A 21-bar balafon.

(Photo courtesy of Kuda Drums, www.kudadrums.com.)

The Least You Need to Know

◆ Drums are a key component of all African music, although which drums are used varies by region and culture.

◆ The most popular African drums include the djembe, ashiko, batá, djun-djun, and talking drum.

◆ The udu drum is actually a clay pot with a hole in its side.

◆ Shakers and metal bells are popular auxiliary instruments in most African cultures.

◆ The balafon and the gyil are the African equivalent of the marimba and xylophone.

Middle Eastern Percussion

In This Chapter

- ◆ Exploring the music of the Middle East
- ◆ Playing the doumbek and other Middle Eastern drums
- ◆ Discovering tambourines and finger cymbals

The next stop on our world music tour is the Middle East, from Arabia to the Mediterranean to the lands of Mesopotamia and Turkey. That includes a lot of different musical cultures that share some very similar percussion instruments.

Understanding the Music of the Middle East

The Middle East is the birthplace of civilization and home to some of the first documented music. While the Middle East gave birth to the music that eventually evolved into what we know as Western music, it also has a rich musical tradition of its own. And, say what you will, Middle Eastern music sounds a whole lot different from the Western music we listen to today.

Exploring Regional Music

What we call Middle Eastern music includes the music of four separate cultures: Arabic, Turkish, Persian, and Israeli. While all Middle Eastern music shares a similar tonal and rhythmic tradition, there are important differences between each of the four major regions.

Arabian music is a mix of native music from local tribes and the music of all the other peoples of the Arabic world. It has also been influenced by the peoples with which the Arabs have traded and interacted—the ancient Greeks, Persians, Kurds, Turks, Indians, Somalis, and the like. There is even, in later Arabic music, a European influence.

What we call Persian music is the traditional music of Iran and other Persian- or Farsi-speaking countries. Classical Persian music is heavily improvised. Composition is based on a series of modal scales and tunes, much as with Arabian and Turkish music. Musicians learn a repertoire of more than 200 series of musical phrases called *radif*.

Turkish music has strong European influences, incorporating elements from Western Europe, Central Asia, Greece, the Arabic peninsula, Persia, and throughout the Ottoman Empire. The music itself is tonally and rhythmically complex, with odd time signatures (5/4, 7/8, and the like) relatively common. That said, Turkish music is probably most familiar of all Middle Eastern music to Western ears.

Israeli music doesn't have the same roots as other Middle Eastern music; remember, the modern country itself didn't exist prior to 1947. That means that all Israeli music is, by definition, immigrant music, derived from the many cultures from which the Jewish state was founded. Influences include traditional Hebrew religious music, Russian folk music, Eastern European klezmer music, and Arabic music. The result is a musical stew with its own particular musical characteristics.

Understanding Middle Eastern Rhythms

Middle Eastern music, like the music of African and India, is more rhythmically complex than the common 4/4 meter of Western music. Much of this music is based on a series of rhythmic modes. These are complex patterns that are repeated over and over again in the course of a performance, typically on a drum or percussion instrument of some sort.

For example, Safi al-Din, a thirteenth-century music theorist and poet, outlined eight of these rhythmic modes. In this system, the uppercase O indicates the initial or accented beat; the lowercase o represents an unaccented note, optionally sounded; the x represents the final note, always sounded; and the period or dot indicates the final note, not sounded—kind of a silent separator.

```
Oo.Oo.Ooo.O.Ooo.  (3+3+4+2+4)

Oo.Oo.O.Oo.Oo.O.  (3+3+2+3+3+2)

O.OxO.OxO.OxO.Ox  (2+2+2+2+2+2+2+2)

Ooo.Ooo.O.O.O.O.O.Ooo.  (4+4+2+2+2+2+2+2+4)

O.O.O.O.O.O  (2+2+2+2+2+2)

O.Oo.O.Oo.  (2+3+2+3)

Ooo.Oo.Oo.O.  (4+3+3+2)

O...O.O...O...O.O...  (4+2+4+4+2+4)
```

Using this playing system, the first rhythmic mode sounds something like this:

```
BOOM bam <rest> BOOM bam <rest> BOOM bam bam <rest> BOOM
<rest> BOOM bam bam <rest>
```

And repeat—over and over again.

These rhythmic modes are played over a traditional Western time signature, which creates some very sophisticated polyrhythms. The most widely used time signature in Middle Eastern music is 6/8, with 3/4 and 2/4 heard on occasion.

Playing Middle Eastern Drums

Middle Eastern music is played on a few popular types of drums. These drums— or similar instruments—are common across all Middle Eastern cultures.

Doumbek

The most popular Middle Eastern drum is the *doumbek*, a goblet-shaped drum similar to the African djembe. If you've ever seen a belly dancer in a Middle Eastern restaurant, you've at least heard the doumbek, accompanying the dancer. The doumbek produces a mix of crisp high tones with soothing, resonant bass tones. It's a versatile instrument.

Pro Tip
Learn more about the djembe in Chapter 13.

All doumbeks produce a low bass sound when struck in the middle of the head, and a higher treble sound when struck around the rim. That said, the precise sound that comes out of a doumbek depends on the individual instrument's size, shape, and head. All things being equal, larger drums produce lower tones; those with narrow necks have more resonance.

A Remo doumbek.

(Photo courtesy of Remo, Inc.)

A doumbek's shell can be wood, ceramic, or metal. Ceramic doumbeks have the warmest sound; metal doumbeks (made from aluminum or copper) have a louder, crisper high tone. The head can be made of calfskin, goatskin, fishskin, or plastic; again, natural heads make for a warmer sound.

Grace Note

I use the term *doumbek* somewhat generically, since similar goblet-shaped drums go by different names in different cultures. In Egypt, it's called the *tablah* (not to be confused with the Indian *tabla*). In Turkey and Israel, it's the *darbuka*. In Lebanon and Syria, it's the *derbakeh*. And in Iran, it's the *tombak* or *zarb*. Different names, same instrument.

You play the doumbek while standing, by holding it under one arm, or while sitting, by placing it horizontally on your lap or vertically between your knees. You can play three main notes on the doumbek:

- **Doum:** A deep, resonating bass sound. Use your dominant hand to strike near the center of the head with your palm and fingers. This note is notated as *D*.

- **Tek:** A higher-pitched, ringing sound played with your dominant hand. Strike near the edge of the head with just your fingertips, almost like a rimshot. A tek is notated as *T*.

- **Ka:** An unaccented note. This note is similar to the tek, but played with your secondary hand. A ka is notated as a lower-case *k*.

So if you're right handed, hold the doumbek under your left arm horizontally, so that the head is toward your right. Use your right hand to play the louder doum and tek notes, and your left hand to play the ka notes.

Experienced doumbek players can produce a number of other tones as well. These include the slap (a doum with cupped fingers), the trill (lightly tap three fingers in rapid succession on the rim), and the roll (rapidly alternating teks and kas).

The doumbek is used to play many traditional rhythms. The most popular of these rhythms include the *ayyoub*, *beledi* (or *baladii*), *chiftitelli* (or *ciftitelli*), *maqsoum* (or *maqsuum*), *masmoudi*, and *saidi* (or *sayyidii*), all notated in the following table.

> **Pro Tip**
>
> The rhythms in the table are just the basic forms of each beat. Experienced players will "fill in the gaps" with additional notes, much the way a Western jazz drummer plays ghost notes on the snare drum.

Doumbek Rhythms

Rhythm	As played
Ayyoub	
	D k D T
Beledi	
	D D T D T

Rhythm	As played
Chiftitelli	D T T D D T
Maqsoum	D T T D T
Masmoudi	D D T D T T
Saidi	D T D D T

Tar

The *tar* is a small, single-headed frame drum, about 14 inches in diameter, much like a tambourine without jingles. The frame is made from wood; the head is typically animal skin, although synthetics heads are becoming more common.

A Remo tar.

(Photo courtesy of Remo, Inc.)

To play the tar, hold the instrument vertically in one hand and strike it with the palm and fingers of the opposing hand. There are four primary tones you can create:

◆ **Doum:** A bass sound, similar to the doum on the doumbek. Strike the head with the ring finger about halfway between the middle and the rim. Alternatively, you can strike it with the thumb or palm of your hand.

◆ **Tak:** A higher, more accented sound. Strike at the edge of the head with the tip of your ring finger.

◆ **Ka:** A sound similar but weaker than the tak. Use the ring finger of the holding hand to strike the head near the rim.

◆ **Pa:** A closed or muted sound. Use all the fingertips of your dominant hand to grab at the center of the head.

Bendir

The *bendir* is another small frame drum, similar in size and construction to the tar, but with a simple snare mechanism underneath the single head. The snare typically consists of two to four gut strands with a permanent tension; the snares aren't adjustable, nor can they be turned off.

The addition of the snares gives the bendir more of a "buzzy" sound than the tar. As with the tar, hold the instrument vertically in one hand and play it with the palm and fingers of the opposite hand. The same doum, tak, ka, and pa techniques apply.

A Remo bendir.

(Photo courtesy of Remo, Inc.)

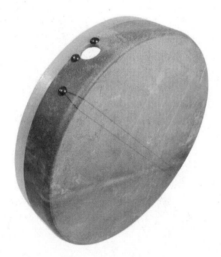

Discovering Other Middle Eastern Percussion

Middle Eastern percussion is almost exclusively hand percussion. Few instruments are hit with a stick or mallet; it's all about the hands.

Tambourine

Add jingles to a tar and you get a *tambourine*, which is essential to all Middle Eastern music. Traditional Middle Eastern tambourines have wood frames and have animal skin heads.

You play a tambourine different in Middle Eastern music than you do in Western music. Hold the drum in one hand in such a way as the middle, ring, and pinky fingers can strike jingles. Then use your dominant hand to produce the following three tones:

Grace Note

Learn more about playing the tambourine in a concert setting in Chapter 7.

- ◆ **Doum:** Strike the head with the first finger.

- ◆ **Tak:** Strike the head with the ring finger.

- ◆ **Pa:** Strike the head with all the fingertips together.

- ◆ **Tik:** Strike a jingle with any finger from either hand.

Riq

The *riq* is a type of tambourine used in Arabic music. It differs from the standard tambourine by having fewer but larger jingles. It is played with your hands, using the same techniques as for the tambourine.

A riq from Remo.

(Photo courtesy of Remo, Inc.)

Finger Cymbals

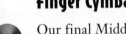

Our final Middle Eastern percussion instrument isn't a drum, it's a set of small cymbals, called *finger cymbals*. As the name implies, these are miniature cymbals, about 2 inches in diameter, that can be (but don't have to be) played with your fingers.

Finger cymbals are made from brass, and are thicker than you'd think they'd be. They produce a piercing bell-like tone when struck together. Finger cymbals are sometimes called *zils*.

A set of finger cymbals from Latin Percussion.

(Photo courtesy of Latin Percussion.)

There are two ways to play finger cymbals. With the traditional method, employed by belly dancers the world over, you hold the two cymbals in one hand (one strapped to your thumb, the other to your middle finger), and clash them together face on. With the Western method, used in orchestral music, you hold one cymbal in each hand, each dangling downward from the strap, and strike the rims together in an upward and downward movement. This second method produces more of a clear tone than the belly dancer's method, and is the preferred technique for "serious" music.

The Least You Need to Know

◆ Middle Eastern music is a mix of local styles and region-wide influences, and is more rhythmically complex than traditional Western music.

◆ The most common percussion instrument in Middle Eastern music is the doumbek, a goblet drum that produces both low and high tones.

◆ Other Middle Eastern drums are frame drums—like tambourines without the jingles.

◆ The tambourine itself is a popular percussion instrument in the region, as are finger cymbals.

Indian Percussion

In This Chapter

- ◆ Find out all about the rhythmically complex music of India

- ◆ Learn how to play the tabla—and the bol rhythms

- ◆ Discover other Indian percussion instruments

India is a strange and foreign land to most Americans, but it's a country rich in its musical traditions. Indian music is diverse and complex, and its percussion instruments exotic yet somehow familiar. Read on to learn more.

Discovering the Music of India

As foreign as Indian culture is to us, the country has one of the world's oldest musical traditions; the country's classical music (*marga*) dates back to the Indus Valley civilization (3300–1700 B.C.E.). This is music with a long history—at least as old as that of the music of the Middle East.

In terms of melody and harmony, most Indian music is based around a single melody line (called a *raga*) played over a fixed drone. Indian music uses a 12-note scale, like Western music, but it's a just tuning, not a tempered one, so it sounds a little "off" to Western ears.

It's the rhythm that we're interested in, of course, and this rhythm is quite interesting. The rhythmic pattern of an Indian composition is called the *tala* (literally, "clap"). The tala is similar to the meter or time signature in Western music, but structurally more sophisticated. In essence, the tala is a long and complex rhythmic pattern that is repeated over and over throughout the composition. This pattern is typically played by various percussion instruments, such as the tabla. Other instruments then play melodies and harmonies over the constant tala.

Grace Note _____

Just tuning is derived from simple ratios between frequencies. *Tempered* tuning (sometimes called *equal temperament*) tweaks just tuning so that every pair of adjacent notes has an identical frequency ratio. With tempered tuning, the octave is divided into 12 equal parts; with just tuning, the same twelve notes aren't always the same interval from one another.

Grace Note _____

The most common tala is the *tintal*, which has a cycle of 16 beats divided into 4 bars. Learn how to play this tala in the "Playing a Tala" section later in this chapter.

The most popular talas include the following:

♦ Dadra, with 6 beats divided 3+3

♦ Dipchandi, with 14 beats divided 3+4+3+4

♦ Ektal, with 12 beats divided 3+3+3+3

♦ Kaharba, with 8 beats divided 4+4

♦ Rupak, with 7 beats divided 3+2+2

♦ Tintal, with 16 beats divided 4+4+4+4

Introducing the Tabla

The most common percussion instrument in Indian music is the *tabla*. This is a pair of drums, consisting of a small, right-hand drum called the *dayan* and a larger, left-hand drum called the *bayan*. The dayan is the treble and the bayan the bass; they both can be tuned to specific pitches.

A pair of tablas; the metal bayan is on the left, the wood dayan on the right.

(Photo courtesy of Suruthilaya, Inc., www.suruthilaya.ca.)

Deconstructing the Tabla

The higher-pitched dayan is cylindrical and stands about 10 inches high. The shell is hardwood (typically teak or rosewood) hollowed out to about half its depth. The head is about about 5 inches in diameter and made from either goat-skin or calfskin.

The lower-pitched bayan is a small kettle drum. The shell is typically made from brass, copper, aluminum, or steel, although some are made from clay. Like the dayan, the bayan's head is typically goatskin.

Both tablas have a large black spot in the middle of the head. This spot, called the *gaab* or *siyahi*, is made from a thick paste of gum, soot, and iron fillings. It lowers the pitch of the drum and creates the tabla's characteristic bell-like sound.

Tuning the Tabla

Each tabla is tuned by a single strap of water buffalo hide, which is woven through the edge of the head. Cylindrical blocks of soft wood (called *ghatta*) are placed between the strap and the body of the drum and used to adjust head tension.

The higher-pitched dayan is tuned to either the tonic, dominant (fifth) or sub-dominant (fourth) note of each piece being played. (Indian music doesn't change key, fortunately.) This enables the drum to complement the melody of the piece.

The lower-pitched drum is not tuned to a particular pitch, just to a general low range. The tuning typically doesn't change from song to song.

Playing the Tabla

You play the tabla while sitting on the floor, the drums nestled in two support-ing rings called *adharas*. You play the right-hand dayan with your right hand and the left-hand bayan with your left hand. You seldom see both hands playing on one drum.

Position the tablas in front of your crossed legs, the larger bayan to your left.

(Photograph courtesy of Pablo Bruno D'Amico via the Creative Commons Attribution-Share Alike 2.0 Generic license.)

There are three primary methods of producing a sound on the tabla: open strokes, closed strokes, and harmonic strokes. You use this last technique on the high drum by touching the skin lightly with your middle finger and then striking the head with the index finger.

Playing the low drum is slightly different from playing the high drum. With this drum, you slide or push on the head with the back of your palm while striking the head with your fingers. This creates a glissando-like pitch change when the drum is struck.

Learning the Bols

The tabla is one of the most complex drums in the world, capable of producing 32 different sounds, called *bols*. Patterns are created from combinations of bols, which are represented by mnemonic syllables taught verbally by the tabla teachers to their students.

A complete listing of bols and presentation of tabla technique is not possible here; you need to study with a master tabla player to learn the instrument. That said, the next three tables present some of the most common bols and how to play them. Note that the *gaab* is the black spot in the center of the head; the *kinar* is the edge of the head; and the *sur* is that part of the head between the gaab and the kinar.

The three areas of a tabla head.

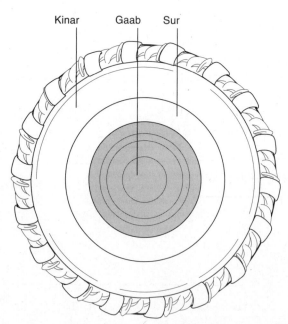

Common dayan (right-hand) bols

Bol	Description
Na	A sharp-sounding stroke. Hit your hand hard against the kinar while simultaneously muting the head with the palm of your hand.
Ta	A sharp, ringing stroke. Hit the head forcefully in the sur area with your index finger.
Ti	A non-resonant stroke. Hit in the dead center of the gaab with your middle finger while muting the drum with the palm of your hand.
Tin	A soft-sounding stroke. Hit at the edge of the gaab while muting the head with the palm of your hand.
Tit	A sharp-sounding strike. Use your index finger to strike hard into the head; don't rebound the finger from the head.
Tr	A right-hand flam with two fingers.
Tu	A soft and resonant stroke. Drop the last three fingers of your hand into the dead center of the gaab without muting the drum.
Tun	An open stroke. Rebound your index finger off the sur.

Common bayan (left-hand) bols

Bol	Description
Ga	A resonant stroke. With the heel of your hand resting about a third of the way from the edge of the drum, "peck" at the sur with either your index or middle finger, recoiling immediately.
Ka	A flat, non-resonant stroke. With the heel of the left hand on the head, rotate your hand to hit the drum across the breadth of the head with all four fingers.
Khat	An explosive stroke. Spread out your fingers as your hand descends to the head, then strike hard on the gaab.

Combination (right- and left-hand) bols

Bol	Description
Dha	Combines the na and ga.
Dhi	Combines the tin and ga.
Dhin	Combines the ta and ga.

You play the combination bols by striking both hands on both drums simultaneously. Try to avoid a flam effect.

Playing a Tala

A rhythmic pattern for tabla—called the *tala*, if you recall—is comprised of a series of different bols. For example, the *tintal* tala looks like this:

```
dha dhin dhin dha/dha dhin dhin dha/na tin tin ta/
ta dhin dhin dha
```

Each tala has its own distinctive beat and pattern of bols. Each Indian song is based on a specific tala, which is repeated throughout the piece of music.

Playing Other Indian Percussion Instruments

While the tabla is the dominant Indian percussion instrument, it's not the only one. There are all manner of drums and bells and tambourines used throughout the various regions; we'll look briefly at the most common ones here.

Note that many of these drums are similar in construction and usage. There are a lot of clay drums with either one or two heads. Most of the two-headed drums are played in a horizontal position, so that both heads are played, much like the two heads of the two tabla drums. In fact, the playing technique of these drums is similar to that of the tabla: The larger head functions as the lower-pitched bayan, while the smaller head functions as the higher-pitched dayan.

Because of these similarities, I won't go into a lot of detail about any specific instrument. Just know that even though the names may be different, the sounds and functionality are similar.

Grace Note

Because of the many different ethnic groups and languages spoken throughout India, the names of individual drums and playing techniques may vary somewhat from region to region and from player to player. I've tried to use the most common names and spellings here, but don't be surprised to see the same instruments named slightly differently in different sources.

The most popular of the Indian percussion instruments include the following:

chenda A cylindrical, two-headed drum, suspended over the player's shoulders. It's held almost vertically and the top head is played with sticks.

chimpta Not a drum, but rather a fire tong (literally used to remove embers from a fire) with brass jingles attached. It's played by slapping the two sides of the tong together.

daff A very large frame drum, about two feet across, mostly played with sticks but sometimes played with hands. When played with sticks, the sticks may or may not have jingles attached.

damaru   A small two-headed hourglass-shaped drum, anywhere from 4 to 10 inches in length and made from either wood or metal. The two heads are laced together with cord, with loose knots near the center of the lacing. The player strikes these knots against both heads to produce a rattling sound. In addition, you can change the pitch of the drum while you are playing it by squeezing the lacing that holds the heads together.

Grace Note

In past times, damaru were sometimes constructed from human skulls(!).

danda   A pair of sticks that are beaten together. The sticks can have jingles attached for a more rattling sound.

dhol   A two-headed barrel drum with both heads played. The smaller, treble head is played with a cane switch, while the larger, bass head is played with a curved cane or stick. The drum itself is held horizontally when played, often suspended from a neck strap.

An Indian dhol drum.

(Photo courtesy of Suruthilaya, Inc., www.suruthilaya.ca.)

dholak   A type of two-headed barrel drum, in many ways just a larger version of the dhol. The larger head has a black tar spot, similar to the tabla's gaab. The dholak is held horizontally and played with either sticks or hands.

ghatam   A large clay pot, similar to the African udu but without the additional resonating hole in the side. It is held with its mouth to the belly of the player and struck with the palms and fingers. The player raises or lowers the pitch of the drum by opening or closing the mouth with his or her stomach. The ghatam is often played in a pair with a mridangam.

Grace Note

Learn more about the udu in Chapter 13.

ghungroo   Ankle bells worn by dancers in northern India. The traditional ghungroo consist of bells woven together on a string. More modern versions have the bells stitched to a padded cushion, which is then strapped to the dancer's foot.

idakka   An hourglass-shaped drum, similar to the damaru. Instead of rattling knotted cords, however, players strike the idakka with a stick. As with the damaru, you can bend the drum's pitch by squeezing the lacing that holds the two heads to the shell.

jal tarang   A set of porcelain bowls filled with water. The size of the bowl and the amount of water inside determines its pitch. The bowls are struck with a light wooden mallet with cotton applied to the beater, to produce a more mellow tone.

Grace Note _____

Learn more about maracas and claves in Chapter 12.

kabbas Hand shakers similar to the Latin American maracas, but with the beads on the outside of the shell. To play it, you hold it in your hand and shake your wrist from side to side.

kanjira A small tambourine, about 7 inches in diameter. The lizard-skin head is stretched over a wooden frame, which has a single metal jingle.

kartal A pair of wooden blocks, similar to claves but with small metal jingles mounted in them. You play the kartal by beating two blocks together.

khol A clay drum with two heads—a small one (4 inches or so) on the right and a larger one (10 inches or so) on the left. The drum is played with the palms and fingers of both hands; the left-hand head is used to tap out bass notes.

The khol, a two-headed clay drum.

(Photo courtesy of Suruthilaya, Inc., www.suruthilaya.ca.)

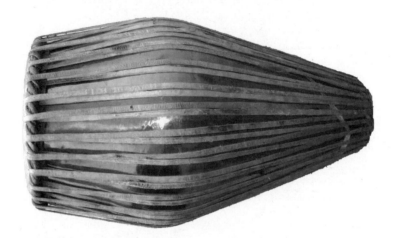

Grace Note _____

Learn more about finger cymbals and doumbeks in Chapter 14.

majira A set of very small cymbals, like Middle Eastern finger cymbals. Like finger cymbals, majira are used in native dance music. They're played by clanging the two cymbals together.

mridangam Also called the *mridang*, a two-headed wooden drum, similar in shape and construction to the clay khol. You play the mridangam by sitting cross-legged on the floor with the instrument on your lap. Your right hand plays the smaller head, while your left hand plays the lower-pitched larger head. The *maddal* is a type of mridangam used primarily in Indian folk music.

An Indian mridangam drum.

(Photo courtesy of Suruthilaya, Inc., www.suruthilaya.ca.)

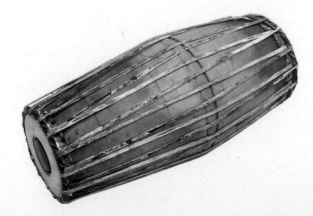

nagari   Also known as *nagara*, *nakara*, *nakir*, or *nagada*, this is a large kettle-drum, anywhere from 1 to 4 feet in diameter. Typically played in pairs, the drums can be made from wood, metal, or clay. They're played with sticks. Nagari—exported to the Middle East and called *naker* or *nakir*—are the ancestors of modern timpani.

A two-foot diameter nagari drum.

(Photo courtesy of Suruthilaya, Inc., www.suruthilaya.ca.)

noot   Also known as the *nout*, this is another clay pot drum, similar to the ghatam. It is played by striking the sides and open mouth with your hands and fingers.

pakhawaj   A north Indian version of the mridangam, a two-headed barrel drum. Both heads are played like the two drums of the tabla, to produce various sounds.

pung   A wooden barrel drum, similar to the clay khol. The two heads of the pung are similar in size.

tavil   A roundish two-headed drum, played horizontally. The right-hand head is played with the hands with metal thimbles placed over the fingers; this creates a sharp and distinct sound. The other head is generally played with a stick, for a contrasting sound.

thanthi panai   A clay pot with a skin stretched over the open mouth. A metal string is attached to the center of the skin and passed through the pot to a small hole drilled in the bottom. The string passes through a series of beads and ties to a tuning peg. When the drum is struck, the beads vibrate.

tumbak   An Indian version of the Middle Eastern doumbek.

Playing technique for all these instruments are similar to techniques you've already learned. Most of the drums (even the clay ones) are played similar to the tabla; the shakers are shaken; and the cymbals are struck together. In this aspect, percussion instruments worldwide share similar techniques.

The Least You Need to Know

- ◆ Indian music is rhythmically complex, comprised of a series of tala rhythms.

- ◆ The most popular Indian instrument is the tabla, which consists of two drums: the lower-pitched bayan and the higher-pitched dayan.

- ◆ Tabla technique involves a series of strokes called bols; all rhythms are constructed from these strokes.

- ◆ Most other Indian instruments serve a similar function as the tabla; many drums are two-headed, thus reproducing the dual tones of the two tabla drums.

Chapter 16

Asian and Indonesian Percussion

In This Chapter

- ◆ Learning about Chinese drums, or *dagu*
- ◆ Discovering Japanese drums, or *taiko*
- ◆ Exploring the drums of Korea, Thailand, and Indonesia

We conclude our look at world percussion by visiting the countries of the Far East—in particular, China, Japan, Korea, Thailand, and Indonesia. There are some interesting instruments here that all percussionists should be aware of, even if they're not part of the everyday repertoire.

I find it interesting that Asian percussion isn't quite as evolved as percussion in nearby India or the almost-nearby Middle East. Drums are mostly used in ceremonial functions, and tend to be large and relatively simple. The music isn't overly rhythmic, so the drums themselves aren't terribly difficult to play—save for the sheer physicality of playing drums so large, of course. In terms of intricacy, then, the Japanese *taiko* is worlds away from the Indian *tabla*.

But that doesn't make Asian percussion any less essential than the percussion of other cultures. While we might not have as ready access to Asian drums themselves (in part because they're so big) and we might not encounter much music that incorporates these instruments, they're still important members of the world percussion family—and so, they are deserving of our attention.

Playing Chinese Drums

Drums are integral in traditional Chinese music, including both Chinese opera and folk music. Even the smallest folk ensembles include one or more drums, along with cymbals and gongs. In traditional Chinese music, drums are used to accompany and pace chanted passages; they also provide rhythmic accompaniment to the acting in Chinese operas.

Even though drums are widely used in all forms of Chinese music, there isn't a lot of variety in terms of instruments. In other words, a Chinese drum is a Chinese drum, more or less.

The most common Chinese drums are bass drums, called *dagu*. They come in two primary types.

The *huapengu* is shaped more or less like a flowerpot and produces a relatively brighter tone. The *datanggu* or *ganggu* is more bowl-shaped and produces a slightly lower pitch. Both are large drums, with heads of 20 inches or so in diameter.

The huapengu Chinese bass drum (left) and the datanggu Chinese bass drum (right).

All dagu are two-headed drums, with wood shells and cowhide heads. The drum is typically suspended on a wooden frame. You play the drum with wood drumsticks, striking midway between the center and edge of the head. In some instances, the shell of the drum is also struck, which produces a sharp, cracking sound.

A smaller type of Chinese drum is the *xiaogu* or *zhangu*. This drum is only about 6 or 7 inches long, with the same broad base as the datanggu. Playing technique is similar, but the resulting tone is louder and higher pitched.

Also common in Chinese music are gongs (*dalo*) and cymbals of various sizes. You'll also find various hand-percussion instruments, such as the *muyu*, a type of woodblock.

Grace Note _____

Learn more about gongs in Chapter 5.

Playing Japanese Drums

Native Japanese folk music was designed to accompany Buddhist rituals, and was rather simple. More complex court music accompanied visitors from China, Korea, and India; this music used percussion instruments as accompaniment.

But the best-known Japanese music is the highly stylized *noh* opera, with sing-ing accompanied by bamboo flutes and drums.

Japanese drums are called *taiko*, and there are a lot of them. Most taiko are two-headed drums and are played with wooden sticks of various sizes called *bachi*. These sticks have no beads; they're straight, long rods.

Unlike drums from most other cultures, Japanese taiko are tensioned quite tightly. This results in a higher pitch than with other drums, and a more cut-ting sound—which is quite unexpected, given the large size of most taiko.

Some of the more common taiko include the following:

- ◆ **Ódaiko.** The largest Japanese drum. These drums are made from a single piece of wood, and range from 6 to 10 *feet* in diameter!

- ◆ **Nagado-daiko.** A large, elongated drum made from a single piece of wood. These drums run from 12 to 36 inches in diameter, and are often played by two drummers.

Remo's nagado-daiko.

(Photo courtesy of Remo, Inc.)

- ◆ **Okedo-daiko.** About six feet long with a three-foot diagonal head. Unlike the similarly large nagado-daiko, this drum is constructed from multiple staves, not a single piece of wood.

- ◆ **Hira-daiko.** A shallow-shelled drum with a boomy sound. These drums come in various sizes, with the larger ones played vertically.

A large hira-daiko from Remo.

(Photo courtesy of Remo, Inc.)

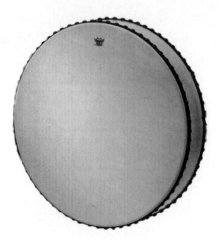

◆ **Shime-daiko.** A small, rope-tensioned drum, about the size of a Western snare drum.

A rope-tensioned shime-daiko.

(Photo courtesy of Remo, Inc.)

Taiko ensembles are common in Japan. These groups typically feature a dozen or more drummers playing taiko of various sizes. The performances are dynamic, due to the sizes of the drums; it's a very physical experience.

Playing Thai Percussion

Thailand is home to a couple of interesting percussion instruments. The first we'll examine is the *klong yao*, a longish wooden drum with a distinct bass tone. It's a single-headed drum with a shell that narrows in the middle; the head size varies from 8 to 12 inches in diameter. The klong yao is played with the hands.

The second Thai drum of interest is the *klong kaak*, a long, two-headed wood drum. The larger head is typically 8 inches or so in diameter; the smaller head is about 7 inches in diameter. Heads are made of calfskin or goatskin.

Klong kaaks are typically played in pairs, like Latin American bongo drums. One drum is pitched lower than the other. You play both heads of the drums with the palms and fingers.

The klong yao, from Thailand.

(Photo courtesy of Remo, Inc.)

Playing Korean Percussion

Korean music is more elaborate than Chinese and Japanese music. It shows more than a bit of influence from Indian music, due to a medieval trading and religious relationship between the two countries. Much of this music is either court music or military music; there is also a form of Korean opera, where the vocalist is accompanied by a single drummer.

Korean drums are called *buk*. The traditional buk is a shallow wood drum with two animal skin heads; the drums can be of various sizes. The buk can be played with two hands on the head, with one hand on the head and the other beating the side of the drum, or with two drumsticks called *bukchae*.

Grace Note

A large buk is sometimes called a *keunbuk* (big drum).

Similar to the buk is the *yonggo*. This drum is used primarily in military wind-and-percussion music, and is played with two padded sticks.

Another interesting Korean drum is the *janggu*. This is the most popular drum in traditional Korean music. The janggu is a two-headed drum with an hourglass shape. The shell can be made from wood, porcelain, or metal. The drum is held horizontally so that both heads can be played. The higher-pitched right head is typically played with a bamboo mallet (called *yeolchae*); the lower-pitched left head is played with the hand.

The Korean janggu hourglass drum.

Playing Indonesian Percussion

Head over to Indonesia and you find a number of interesting percussion instruments used in the native *Gamelan* ensembles. These ensembles feature a variety of native percussion, wind, and string instruments; some ensembles also feature vocalists. These ensembles typically accompany dances, rituals, and other formal ceremonies.

The primary drum in the Gamelan ensemble is the *kendang*. This is a long, two-headed drum played with both hands or with one hand and a stick. The drum is played horizontally, so that both heads can be struck simultaneously.

Another interesting Indonesian instrument is the *gender*, a *metallophone* with metal bars tuned to precise pitches. You play the gender with two wooden mallets; once a note is struck, you immediately muffle it with the palm of the same hand.

def•i•ni•tion

A **metallophone** is a musical instrument constructed from tuned metal bars, such as the vibraphone or glockenspiel.

Balinese straight-shelled kendang.

Grace Note _____

The kendang differs significantly in construction from region to region. For example, the Bali kendang has a straight shell with both heads the same size, while the shell of the Java kendang tapers from a larger head to a smaller one.

The gender isn't the only Indonesian pitched percussion instrument, however. There is also the *gambang*, a wooden xylophone-like instrument; the *slenthem* and *saron*, two more metallophones similar to the gender; and the *bonang*, a set of fixed-pitch kettle gongs that resembles a collection of metal pots with raised lids. They're interesting instruments, all of them.

A set of Indonesian bonang, a set of fixed-pitch kettle gongs.

(Photo courtesy of Giovanni Sciarrino via the Creative Commons Attribution-ShareAlike 3.0 license.)

Moving beyond the fixed-pitch instruments, our final member of the Indonesian percussion family is the *cheng cheng*, a pair of brass cymbals that are clashed together in the usual fashion. Gamelan ensembles typically have multiple cheng chengs that play intricate interlocking patterns.

And That's Not All ...

There are many more world percussion instruments available than we have space to discuss here. While I admit that this book is Western percussion–centric, that doesn't mean you should limit your study of percussion instruments to those in traditional Western orchestral, marching, and popular music, no more than you should limit your study of cultures and history to that of Western Europe and the Americas. Every part of the world has its own unique and compelling musical culture, all worthy of your interest and study.

You may never be called upon to play a tabla or taiko, but then again, you may. After all, our own musical culture has always been influenced by other musical cultures and will continue to be so in the future. Think how ubiquitous instruments such as congas and bongos have become, even though they're not native to our traditional orchestral and popular music. For that matter, even our most

208 Part 5: The World of Ethnic Percussion

traditional percussion instruments, from the gong to the timpani, originally came from other cultures. The percussion family is continually growing as we reflect the influences of other cultures.

So it's important that you open your eyes and ears to all the different percussion instruments of the world. Yes, you probably should focus your initial attentions on those instruments you're most likely to encounter every day, but that shouldn't stop you from expanding your skill set to include Latin American, African, Indian, Middle Eastern, and Asian playing techniques.

A well-rounded percussionist knows how to play lots of different instruments. That should be reason enough to study the instruments of other cultures. Besides, these instruments—like all percussion instruments—are interesting and fun. You don't know what you're missing until you try it!

The Least You Need to Know

- Chinese drums (dagu) include the huapengu and datanggu bass drums, as well as the smaller xiaogu.

- Japanese drums (taiko) include the large ódaiko, nagado-daiko, hira-daiko, and okedo-daiko, as well as the smaller shime-daiko.

- Thai drums include the single-headed klong yao and double-headed, bongolike kong kaak.

- Indonesian percussion includes the two-headed kendang drum, the gender metallophone, the bonang kettle gongs, and the cheng cheng cymbals.

Glossary

accent   A note played louder or with more emphasis than regular notes.

aerophone   An instrument that produces sound when wind is blown through or around it. Examples include the clarinet and trumpet.

afuche/cabasa   A small ribbed metal cylinder covered by strings of metal beads.

agogo bells   A set of two metal bells, kind of like small cowbells, connected via a curved piece of metal. One bell is smaller than another, so that each bell sounds its own unique (indefinite) pitch.

antique cymbal   See *crotale*.

apiua bell   A small, iron, African bell, about 6 inches long.

ashiko   A goblet-shaped African hand drum similar to the djembe but with a slightly lower pitch.

atsimevu   The tallest African Ewe drum—almost 4½ feet tall.

attack   The initial sound made when you hit a drum or cymbal—as opposed to the ring or "after tone."

auxiliary percussion   Any non-drum, non-cymbal, non-melodic percussion instrument used in an orchestral setting—typically, hand-held percussion instruments.

bachi   Wooden sticks used to play Japanese drums.

backbeat   In 4/4 time, beats two and four, typically played by a drum set drummer on the snare drum.

balafon   A marimba-like instrument from Africa, typically with 17 to 21 wooden bars.

basket shaker   An African shaker constructed from small cane baskets with gourd bottoms and pebbles inside.

bass clef   A clef, used by lower-pitched instruments, that places middle C on the first ledger line above the staff.

bass drum   A large drum that provides the booming bottom tone in an ensemble. In concert use, it is played with mallets on one head; in marching band use, it is played with mallets on both heads; in drum set use, it is played with a foot pedal.

bass drum pedal   The foot pedal used to play a bass drum in a drum set.

batá   A two-headed Nigerian hand drum with one head larger than the other.

batter head   The head of the drum that is struck, typically the top head.

bayan   The large left-hand Indian tabla drum.

bead   The tip of the drumstick.

beat   Any pulsing unit of musical time.

bell   1. The round, raised center of a cymbal. 2. Generically, a piece of metal with one closed and one open end, such as a cowbell.

bell lyre   See *glockenspiel.*

bell tree   A small "tree" made up of nested metal bells or bowls, each tuned to a definite pitch.

bells   See *glockenspiel.*

bendir   A small, Middle Eastern frame drum with a simple snare mechanism underneath the single head.

boba   The deepest-sounding African Ewe drum.

bol   One of the 32 different sounds produced by the Indian tabla drum.

bongo   A small, high-pitched, single-headed Cuban hand drum, typically played in pairs.

bonang   A set of Indonesian fixed-pitch kettle gongs that resembles a collection of metal pots with raised lids.

bow   That part of a cymbal that reaches from the bell to the edge.

brushes   Fan-shaped devices made of wire strands attached to a handle, often used for playing soft jazz and ballads on a drum set.

buk   A traditional two-headed Korean drum.

bukchae   Korean drumsticks.

Burton grip   A four-mallet melodic percussion grip (two mallets are held in each hand); a variation on the traditional grip but with a wider interval range. The grip was developed by jazz vibraphonist Gary Burton.

butt   The end of the drumstick opposite from the bead.

cabasa   A type of shaker constructed from a hollow gourd with strings of beads around the outside.

Cajón   A wooden Peruvian box drum that sounds a low bass note.

castanet   A small, hand-held instrument consisting of two wooden or plastic halves that are clicked together.

chendra   A cylindrical, two-headed Indian drum, played with sticks.

cheng cheng   A pair of brass cymbals used in Indonesian Gamelan ensembles.

chime tree   See *wind chimes.*

chimes   A melodic percussion instrument constructed from long, vertically mounted metal tubes.

chimpta   An Indian percussion instrument constructed from a fire tong with brass jingles attached.

China cymbal   A cymbal with an upturned edge, typically played upside down for a trashy ride or crash sound.

chord   Three or more notes played simultaneously.

chordophone   An instrument that produces sound when a struck or plucked string vibrates. Examples include the piano and harpsichord.

chromatic scale   A scale containing 12 equal divisions of the octave—all the white keys and black keys within an octave.

clave   1. A Latin percussion instrument consisting of two wooden cylinders struck together. 2. The most basic Latin rhythm, consisting of a 3-2 two-bar pattern.

clef   A graphic symbol placed at the beginning of the staff to indicate the pitch of the notes on the staff.

closed roll   A multiple-stroke roll produced by pressing the stick into the head for multiple bounces. Also called a buzz roll or a press roll.

concert bass drum   A large bass drum played in concert and orchestral music. The drum is typically mounted vertically and played with one or two mallets on a single head.

concert percussion   Percussion instruments played in a concert or orchestral setting.

concert pitch   The actual (nontransposed) pitch of a piece of music; for some instruments (such as the glockenspiel), musicians read their music transposed from concert pitch.

concert toms   A set of four or eight single-headed tom-toms, used in both orchestral and popular music.

conga   1. A deep, single-headed Cuban drum, played by hand. 2. The middle-sized drum in a trio of conga drums.

cowbell   A medium-sized metal bell with one open end, used in Latin American and Western popular music.

crash cymbal   A relatively thin cymbal that, when hit hard, produces a loud burst of sound with quick decay.

crescendo   Gradually louder.

crotale   A small (4 inches or so) round metal disk that produces a piercing bell-like sound with a definite pitch. Crotales are typically played in one- or two-octave sets.

cuica   A Latin American single-headed friction drum with a small wooden dowel attached to (and through) the underside of the goatskin head.

cymbal   A thin piece of round metal that vibrates when hit with a stick or mallet.

daff   A very large Indian frame drum, about two feet across.

dagu   Chinese bass drums.

dalo   A Chinese gong.

damaru   A small two-headed hourglass-shaped Indian drum.

danda   An Indian percussion instrument consisting of a pair of sticks that are beaten together.

darbuka   See *doumbek*.

datanggu   A bowl-shaped Chinese bass drum.

dayan   The small right-hand Indian tabla drum.

decrescendo   Gradually softer.

definite pitch instrument   A percussion instrument that produces tones that correspond to specific frequencies or musical pitches. Examples include the xylophone, marimba, vibraphone, glockenspiel, and timpani.

derbakeh   See *doumbek*.

dhol   A two-headed Indian barrel drum.

dholak   A two-headed Indian barrel drum, a larger version of the dhol.

djembe   A popular goblet-shaped, single-headed African hand drum.

djun-djun   A two-headed bass drum typically used to accompany the djembe in West African drum ensembles.

djun-djun bell   An African version of the Latin American cowbell, typically attached to the side of a djun-djun drum and played with an iron striker.

dominant   The fifth degree of a scale, a perfect fifth above the tonic.

doumbek   A goblet-shaped, single-headed Middle Eastern drum, similar to the African djembe.

doundoumba   A large African djun-djun drum.

downbeat   The major beats in a measure; in 4/4 time, the downbeats are 1, 2, 3, and 4.

drum   A hollow body percussion instrument with a membrane head of some sort stretched over the top.

drum circle   A group of people, typically not professional musicians, gathered into a circle for the express purpose of playing drums and other percussion instruments.

drum corps   A smaller, specialized, more highly skilled variation of the marching band.

drum set   A kit of drums, including a snare drum, a bass drum, tom-toms, and cymbals, typically played in popular music.

drum throne   See *throne*.

drumstick   A long wooden stick, typically with one beaded end, used to strike a drum or cymbal.

dundun   See *djun-djun*.

dunun   See *djun-djun*.

dynamics   Varying degrees of loud and soft.

edge   The outer rim of a cymbal or drumhead.

electrophone   An instrument that produces sound electronically. Examples include drum machines, MIDI instruments, and computer loops.

Ewe drums   The family of drums found in Ghana drumming ensembles. Popular Ewe drums include the kroboto, kaganu, kidi, sogo, atsimevu, and boba.

fill   A drum set pattern played, typically on the toms, at the end of one musical phrase leading into the next phrase.

finger cymbals   A set of miniature brass cymbals, about 2 inches in diameter, used in Middle Eastern music.

flag   That part of the note that extends sideways from the note stem and is used to designate 8th, 16th, and 32nd notes. An 8th note has one flag, a 16th note has two, and a 32nd note has three.

flam   A grace note played almost simultaneously with the main note, from hand to hand.

flexatone   An auxiliary percussion instrument that consists of a small sheet of flexible metal attached at one end to a handle; two wooden balls are mounted on either side of the sheet. The balls are hit against the metal piece, which is bent with the player's thumb to create a "bo-ing" type of effect.

floor tom   See *large tom*.

French grip   A grip used in timpani and melodic percussion playing where the thumbs are placed on top of the mallets.

gaab   The large black spot in the middle of the head of an Indian tabla drum.

gambang   A wooden xylophone-like instrument from Indonesia.

Gamelan   A type of Indonesian musical ensemble that features a variety of native percussion, wind, and string instruments.

ganggu   See *datanggu*.

gankogui   The African predecessor of the Latin agogo bell.

gender   An Indonesian metallophone with metal bars tuned to precise pitches.

German grip   A grip used in timpani and melodic percussion playing where the thumbs are placed on the side of the mallets; similar to the snare drummer's matched grip.

ghatam   An Indian percussion instrument constructed from a large clay pot; similar to the African udu.

ghost note   A note played very lightly in comparison to others.

ghungroo   Ankle bells worn by dancers in northern India.

glissando   A mechanism for getting from one pitch to another, playing every single pitch between the two notes as smoothly as possible.

glockenspiel   A high-pitched melodic percussion instrument with small metal bars and a two-and-a-half- to three-octave range. It is played horizontally in orchestral situations and vertically in marching bands and drum corps.

gong   A large, round, metallic, cymbal-like instrument with an in-turned edge. Technically, a gong has a raised center area and produces a definite pitch; what we commonly call a gong is actually a tam-tam, which lacks the raised center and has an indefinite pitch.

grace note   One or more notes, played lightly and quickly, that precede a main note.

guiro   A Latin American instrument traditionally constructed from a cylindrical gourd with grooves cut around its circumference; sound is produced when a stick is scraped across the grooves.

gyil   A small African xylophone-type instrument, typically tuned to a pentatonic scale.

hand cymbals   In marching and orchestral music, two cymbals held vertically and clashed together to create a "crash" sound.

harmony   The sound of tones in combination; also used to refer to the accompanying parts behind the main melody.

hi-hat   Two smaller cymbals in a drum set that are closed together via a pedal and played with both the foot and with sticks.

hira-daiko   A shallow-shelled Japanese drum.

huapengu   A flowerpot-shaped Chinese bass drum.

idakka   An Indian hourglass-shaped drum, similar to the damaru.

idiophone   An instrument without a head whose entire body vibrates when struck. Examples include the xylophone, bells, and cymbals.

indefinite pitch instrument   A percussion instrument that produces tones that do not correspond to specific frequencies or musical pitches, and instead produces a general sound with multiple frequencies. Examples include most drums (excluding timpani) and cymbals.

interval   The distance between two pitches or notes.

interval tuning   The process of tuning a timpani using a starting tone and relative pitch.

itotele   The alto or tenor batá drum.

iya   The bass batá drum.

jal tarang   A set of porcelain bowls filled with water, used as a percussion instrument in Indian music.

janggu   A two-headed Korean drum with an hourglass shape.

jazz   A style of music that incorporates and encourages improvisation.

jingle bells   See *sleigh bells.*

kabbas   An African hand shaker, similar to the maracas, but with the beads on the outside of the shell.

kaganu   A small, high-pitched African Ewe drum.

kanjira   A small Indian tambourine with a single metal jingle.

kartal   A pair of wooden blocks used in Indian music, similar to claves but with small metal jingles mounted in them.

kendang   The long, two-headed drum used in Indonesian Gamelan ensembles.

kenkeni   A small African djun-djun drum.

kettledrum   The twelfth-century predecessor to the modern-day *timpani.*

keunbuk   A large Korean buk drum.

khol   A two-headed Indian clay drum.

kidi   A mid-size African Ewe drum.

kinar   The edge of the head on a tabla drum.

klong kaak   A long, two-headed, wooden Thai drum.

klong yao   A long, single-headed, wooden Thai drum.

kroboto   A squat, lower-pitched African Ewe drum.

lagerphone   An Australian percussion instrument constructed from a large wooden stick affixed with metal jingles.

large tom   A tom-tom positioned to the right of the bass drum, parallel with the head of the snare drum, in a drum set.

lug   The casing that is attached to a drum shell and accepts a tuning rod.

maddal   A type of mridangam used primarily in Indian folk music.

majira   A set of very small Indian cymbals, like Middle Eastern finger cymbals.

mallet   A beater used for timpani, melodic percussion, and some drums, typically with a handle made from wood or plastic and a metal, hard plastic, rubber, or yarn- or felt-covered head.

mallet percussion   Definite pitch percussion instruments that have multiple bars arranged like a piano keyboard. Examples include the xylophone, marimba, vibraphone, and glockenspiel.

maraca   A small dried gourd with seeds inside; typically held by the handle and shaken.

marimba   The lowest-pitched melodic percussion instrument, constructed of wood or synthetic bars over a four- to five-and-a-half-octave range.

mark tree   See *wind chimes*.

martillo   A popular bongo pattern, also known as the "hammer."

matched grip   A snare drum/drum set grip where both hands share an identical grip.

measure   A group of beats, indicated by the placement of bar lines on the staff.

melodic percussion   See *mallet percussion*.

melody   The combination of tone and rhythm in a logical sequence.

membranophone   An instrument with a head that vibrates when struck. Examples include drums and timpani.

metallophone   An instrument constructed of metal bars. Examples include the vibraphone and glockenspiel.

mridang   See *mridangam*.

mridangam   A two-headed Indian drum, similar in shape and construction to the clay khol but with a wood shell.

Musser grip   A non-crossing four-mallet (two in each hand) melodic percussion grip. The grip was developed by marimbist Clair Omar Musser.

muyu   A Chinese woodblock.

nagada   See *nagari*.

nagado-daiko   A large, elongated Japanese drum made from a single piece of wood.

nagara   See *nagari*.

nagari   A large Indian kettledrum, anywhere from one to four feet in diameter.

nakara   See *nagari*.

ngoma   A tall, single-headed African drum that produces a sound similar to the conga drum.

noot   An Indian clay pot drum, similar to the ghatam.

note   A symbol used to indicate the duration and pitch of a sound, as in whole notes, half notes, and quarter notes.

note head   The round filled or hollow part of the note that designates the note's pitch.

note stem   That part of a note extending up or down from the note head. All notes except whole notes have stems.

nout   See *noot*.

oconcolo   A soprano batá drum.

octave   Two pitches, with the same name, located 12 half-steps apart.

ódaiko   The largest Japanese drum, made from a single piece of wood up to 10 feet in diameter.

okedo-daiko   A Japanese drum made from six-foot-long wooden staves.

open roll   A series of 32nd notes played with double strokes.

orchestra bells   See *glockenspiel*.

pakhawaj   A north Indian version of the mridangam, a two-headed barrel drum.

pandeiro   A Brazilian tambourine, but with heavier, convex metal jingles.

paradiddle   Four notes of equal duration played with either a RLRR or a LRLL sticking. A double paradiddle consists of six notes with either an RLRLRR or LRLRLL sticking.

percussion   The family of instruments that produce sound when you hit, beat, crash, shake, roll, scratch, rub, twist, or rattle them.

percussion ensemble   A performing group consisting of various percussion instruments.

percussion staff   One of two special staffs used to notate indefinite pitch percussion instruments. The percussion staff does not denote individual pitches and can have either one or five lines.

Percussive Arts Society (PAS)   The premier organization for drummers and percussion educators. Its website is located at www.pas.org.

phrase   Within a piece of music, a segment that is unified by rhythms, melodies, or harmonies and that comes to some sort of closure; typically composed in groups of 2, 4, 8, 16, or 32 measures.

pitch   The highness or lowness of a tone.

polyrhythm   Two or more rhythms played simultaneously, or against each other.

popular percussion   Percussion instruments played in popular music or drum circles.

pung   A wooden barrel drum from India, similar to the clay khol.

quads   A group of four tenor drums.

quinto   The smallest drum in a set of three conga drums.

quints   A group of five tenor drums.

radif   The repertoire of more than 200 musical phrases found in classical Persian music.

ratchet   An auxiliary percussion instrument consisting of a gear that clicks against thin pieces of wood when turned with a handle.

relative pitch   The ability to recognize a pitch by mentally establishing a relationship between that pitch and a previous pitch.

repinique   A small, double-headed Brazilian drum, played with sticks or one stick and one hand.

resonant head   The front or bottom head of a drum that is *not* struck; so named because it resonates when the batter head is hit. Also called the snare head.

resonator   A long metal tube placed beneath the bars on some mallet percussion instruments. The tube acoustically amplifies the sound and helps the bar to resonate longer.

rhythm   The organization of sound in time; the arrangement of beats and accents in music.

rhythmic notation   Special musical notation, typically used for cymbals and similar percussion instruments, that replaces traditional note heads with *x*'s and *o*'s.

ride cymbal   In a drum set, a large, relatively heavy cymbal that is used to keep time via a repeating "ride" pattern.

riding tom   See *small tom.*

rim   The wood or metal hoop that sits on top of the edge of the drumhead and attaches the head to the shell.

rimshot   A snare drum technique that involves simultaneously hitting the head and the rim of the drum with the bead and shoulder of the drumstick.

riq   An Arab tambourine with a small number of large jingles.

roll   Several notes played rapidly in succession, typically with two or more strokes on each hand; a roll can be either *open* or *closed.*

Roto Tom   A single-headed drum without a shell that can be tuned to a specific pitch; it is typically played in sets of two or three or more. This drum was developed by Remo, Inc.

rudiment   One of 40 basic rhythmic patterns, as codified by the Percussive Arts Society.

ruff   Two grace notes attached to a main note; the grace notes are played with a double stroke on one hand, while the main note is played with the opposite hand.

samba   An essential Latin pulsing rhythm, usually played on the bass drum, consisting a dotted quarter note followed by an eighth note, repeated.

sandblocks   See *sandpaper blocks*.

sandpaper blocks   A set of woodblocks with sandpaper attached, used to create a scratching sound.

sangban   A medium-sized African djun-djun drum.

saron   An Indonesian metallophone.

shaker   A hollow metal, plastic, or wood tube or ball with small beads or pellets inside that create a rattling sound when shaken.

shekere   An African shaker made from a dried gourd surrounded by a net of beads.

shell   The thin, hollow cylinder that comprises the main body of a drum; shells can be made from solid wood, plies of wood, fiberglass, steel, bronze, or other materials.

shime-daiko   A small rope-tensioned Japanese drum.

shoulder   That part of a drumstick that begins to taper down to the bead.

shuffle   A rhythmic feel based on triplets or a dotted 8th note/16th note pattern.

siyahi   See *gaab*.

sizzle cymbal   A ride cymbal with rivets for a sustained sizzling sound.

slapstick   A long plank of wood with a second, shorter plank connected with a spring hinge; it is used to create a whiplike sound.

sleigh bells   A set of multiple small bells, each with a small clapper inside, typically attached to a wooden handle. It is usually used to create a Christmasy, horse-drawn sleigh effect.

slenthem   An Indonesian metallophone.

small tom   A tom-tom positioned above the bass drum in a drum set.

snare drum   A thin wood or metal-shelled drum with metal wires running alongside the bottom head to produce a crisp sound; the snare drum is used to reinforce the backbeat in rock music.

snare head   The bottom or resonant head on a snare drum.

snare strainer   The assembly that holds and facilitates tuning of the metals snares on a snare drum.

sogo   A mid-sized African Ewe drum, a larger version of the kidi.

splash cymbal   A small (12 inches or smaller), thin, splashy-sounding cymbal.

staff   An assemblage of horizontal lines and spaces that represent different pitches.

steel drum   A pitched, melodic drum, popular in Caribbean music, made from a steel oil drum.

steelpan   See *steel drum*.

Stevens grip   A non-crossing four-mallet melodic percussion grip (two mallets are held in each hand). This variation on the Musser grip was developed by marimbist Leigh Howard Stevens.

subdominant   The fourth degree of the scale, or the chord built on the fourth degree (IV).

sur   That part of the head of a tabla drum between the middle (gaab) and outer edge (kinar).

surdo   A large double-headed drum that provides the bass voice in much Brazilian music.

suspended cymbal   In orchestral playing, a cymbal mounted horizontally on a stand and played with mallets or sticks.

suspension mount   A type of tom-tom or concert bass drum holder that doesn't attach directly to the drum's shell; instead, a suspension mount attaches the drum's tuning rods or rim, thus enabling the shell to vibrate more freely.

syncopation   An accent on an unexpected beat—or the lack of an accent on an expected beat.

tabla   The most popular Indian drums, actually consisting of two drums of different sizes.

tablah   See *doumbek*.

taiko   Japanese drums.

tala   The rhythmic pattern of an Indian composition.

talking drum   An hourglass-shaped Nigerian drum. The player makes the drum "talk" by squeezing the tensioning cords that connect the top and bottom heads.

tam-tam   A gong that has an indefinite pitch.

tamborim   A small, single-headed frame drum, about 6 inches in diameter, used in Latin American music.

tambourine   A small round frame drum with metal jingles embedded into the wooden frame; it can be either headed or headless. Originally a Middle Eastern instrument, it is now used in Western orchestral and popular music.

tar   A small, single-headed, Middle Eastern frame drum, much like a tambourine without jingles.

tavil   A roundish, two-headed Indian drum.

temple blocks   A set of five hollow wooden or plastic blocks with slits through the middle, each with its own (indefinite) pitch.

tempo   The rate of speed at which beats are played in a song.

tenor drums   A set of single-headed tom-toms used in marching bands and drum corps, typically carried in groups of three or more.

tension rods   The threaded screwlike pieces that fit through a drum's hoop and screw into the lugs; tension lugs are used to adjust the tension of a drum head.

Thanthi Panai   A clay pot with a skin stretched over the open mouth, used in Indian music.

throne   The seat in a drum set.

throwoff   The assembly that moves the wire snares next to or away from the snare drum's snare head.

thumb roll   A roll played with the thumb on a headed tambourine.

thundersheet   A thin sheet of metal, anywhere from two to three feet wide and high, hung vertically from a stand. It is used to create the sound of thunder.

timbale   A shallow, single-headed drum used in Latin American music. It is typically played in pairs with thin dowel-like sticks.

time signature   The fractionlike notation that indicates the basic meter of a song. The upper number indicates how many beats are in a measure, and the bottom number indicates the type of note that receives one beat.

timpani   Large copper-shelled drums that can be tuned to definite pitches. Timpani sound at the lower end of the percussion range, and are typically played in groups of two, four, or five drums.

tom mount   The apparatus that attaches the tom-tom to a stand or tom holder.

tom-tom   Sometimes known just as a "tom," this drum produces a low-pitched sound; smaller toms produce higher pitches.

tombak   See *doumbek*.

tonic   The primary note in a scale or key; the first degree of a scale or a chord is built on that degree (I).

traditional grip 1. A snare drum/drum set grip where the left hand holds the stick palm up, with the stick between the third and fourth fingers and between the thumb and index finger. 2. A four-mallet melodic percussion grip (two mallets are held in each hand) where the two mallets cross over each other in the palm of the hand.

treble clef A clef, used by higher-pitched voices and instruments, that places middle C on the first ledger line below the staff.

triangle An auxiliary percussion instrument constructed from steel rod bent into a three-sided, triangular shape. It produces a high-pitched "ding" when struck with a metal beater.

trio A group of three tenor drums.

triplet A group of three notes performed in the space of two.

tubular bells See *chimes*.

tumbadora See *tumbao (1)*.

tumbak An Indian version of the Middle Eastern doumbek.

tumbao 1. The largest drum in a set of three conga drums. 2. A conga technique created by rocking between the palm and fingertips of the hand; it is used to play the tumbao pattern, common in salsa music.

udu A Nigerian hand drum made from a clay pot with an extra hole in the side.

vibes See *vibraphone*.

vibraphone A melodic percussion instrument with metal bars (and a three-octave range) and an electric motor that produces a vibrato-like sound.

vibraslap An auxiliary percussion instrument constructed from a small wooden box and a wooden ball, connected via a metal rod. The ball is slapped toward the box, which contains loose-fitting metal pins inside, to create a sustained rattle.

wind chimes A set of small metal or wooden tubes that create a sound when struck against each other. Wind chimes used as orchestral instruments are more precisely called chime trees or mark trees.

woodblock A small rectangular piece of solid wood, played with a hard mallet or stick.

xiaogu A small Chinese drum.

xylophone A higher-pitched melodic percussion instrument, constructed from wood or synthetic bars over a typical three-octave range.

yonggo A Korean drum used primarily in military wind-and-percussion music.

zarb See *doumbek*.

zhangu See *xiaogu*.

zils See *finger cymbals*.

Into the West: A Short Piece for Percussion Ensemble

Into the West is a short piece for percussion ensemble, written to demonstrate how various orchestral percussion instruments sound when played together in a real-life setting. It can be played by as few as five players, with some doubling of instruments. (For example, one person can play both snare drum and bass drum; another can play both glockenspiel and xylophone.)

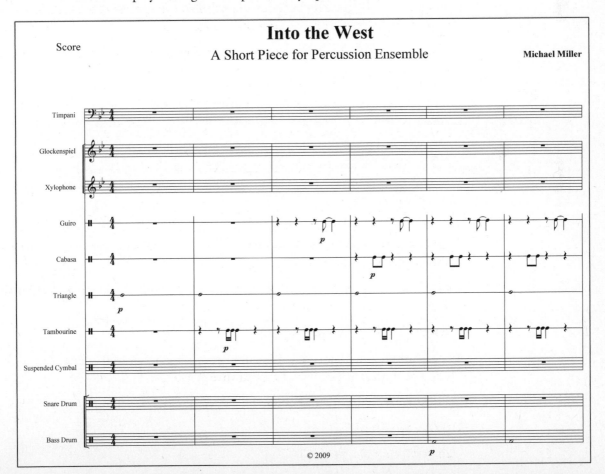

Into the West

Into the West

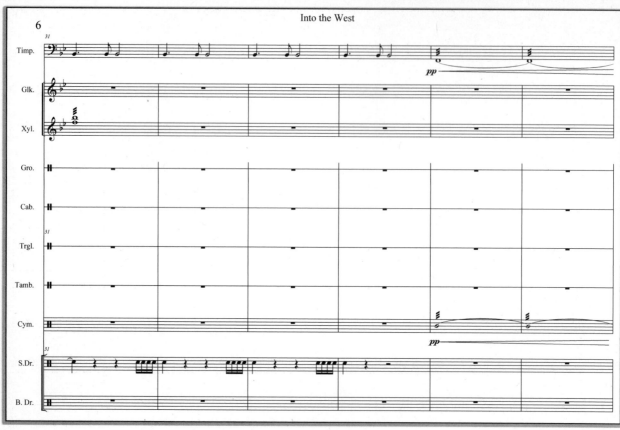

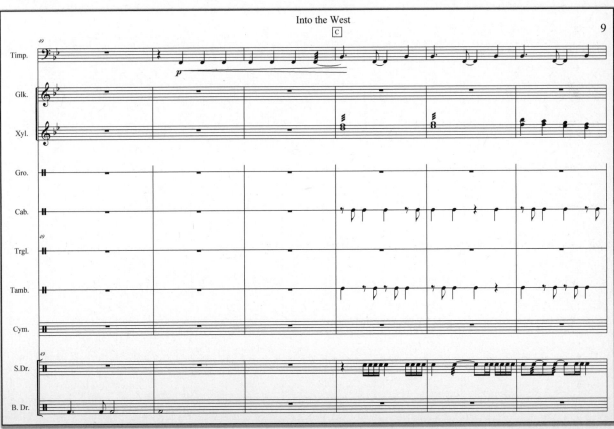

Appendix C

CD Contents

The compact disc accompanying this book contains examples of many of the percussion instruments discussed in the text. Listen to learn what these instruments sound like—and to learn some specific techniques.

1. Introduction
2. Concert snare drum
3. Concert toms
4. Concert bass drum
5. Timpani
6. Suspended cymbal
7. Hand cymbals
8. Gong (tam-tam)
9. Crotales
10. Marimba
11. Xylophone
12. Vibraphone
13. Glockenspiel
14. Chimes
15. Triangle
16. Tambourine
17. Wood block
18. Temple blocks
19. Slapstick
20. Sandpaper blocks
21. Ratchet
22. Vibraslap
23. Flexatone
24. Shaker
25. Sleigh bells
26. Wind chimes
27. Bell tree
28. Thundersheet
29. Drumline (marching percussion section)
30. Marching snare drum
31. Tenor drums
32. Marching bass drums
33. Marching cymbals
34. Drum set
35. Basic drum set beats
36. Conga drums
37. Bongos
38. Timbales
39. Surdo
40. Cuica
41. Cowbell

42. Agogo bells
43. Claves
44. Guiro
45. Castanets
46. Cabasa
47. Maracas
48. Djembe
49. Ashiko
50. Djun-djun
51. Udu

52. Talking drum
53. Shekere
54. Doumbek
55. Finger cymbals
56. Tabla
57. Chinese drums (dagu)
58. Japanese drums (taiko)
59. Summary
60. *Into the West: A Short Piece for Percussion Ensemble*

These recordings were made using Steinberg Cubase 5 and Sony Sound Forge 9 software. Editing and mixing was done using Cubase 5, with CD mastering accomplished with Sony CD Architect. Thanks to Dr. David Schalenberger of the McNally Smith College of Music for providing and playing many of these instruments.

Index

Q

R

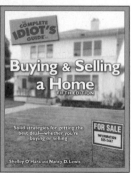
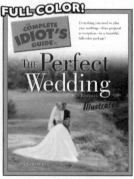
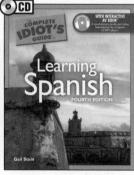

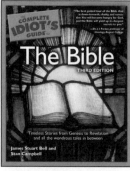
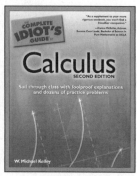

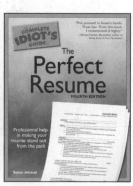
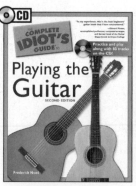

Discover the keys to making great music with these top-selling *Complete Idiot's Guides®* by Michael Miller!

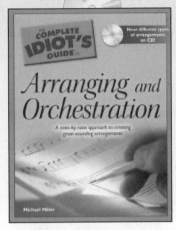

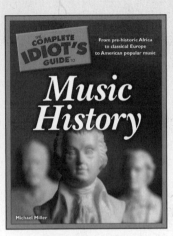

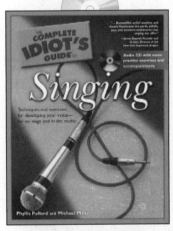

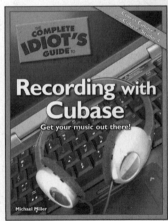